Open Carry

Poems

by Steve Advocate

for my Martec
(of memories)

Steve
5/13/24

stadvo@gmail.com

For Monika

Nature Walk

Look, look, you cry elatedly,
That blue jay up there in the tree,
And deep inside the river, see,
The sleek fish glides so silvery.

You turn to me to share your quick delight—
    Epiphanies as sudden as the swerves
Of hummingbirds, discoveries as bright
    As moon's first step into the empty night . . .

Try as I might to match my eye with yours,
    The only thing my squinting lets me see
Is you, my joy—which well enough suits me
    And offers more than anyone deserves.

Contents

Fairly Personal

T-Rex Under My Pillow

All Kinds of Fun

Diatribes

Because it is

Poems per se

Envoi

Introduction: Sunrise, Sunset

Welcome to the Poet's Brain

Welcome to the poet's brain,
It's free of charge and free from strain,
You'll never even feel the pain—

> *Welcome to the poet's brain.*

Your flag still flies at topmost mast,
Leave *him* to mine the heartbreak past,
To prove that lives and loves don't last—

> *Welcome to the poet's brain.*

Don't try to do the job yourself,
Keep all your cares wrapped up and shelved,
You don't know how they're turned to wealth—

> *Welcome to the poet's brain.*

He is the one who wants to bleed.
If with the blood you find a seed,
Then crush it as you would a weed—

> *Welcome to the poet's brain.*

He's not the man who should be saved,
He swam beyond the whitecap waves
And only wishes you as brave—

> *Welcome to the poet's brain.*

The poet welcomes everyone,
From any stranger to his son,
Who can enjoy this kind of fun—

> *Welcome to the poet's brain.*

He taught the bird of suffering,
Who circles on extended wing,
To light upon his wrist and sing—

> *Welcome to the poet's brain.*

Breathing

through

a long

straw

from deep

down

breathing

freedom's

long drawn

air

chest heavy

with the weight

of suffocation

from time

to time

tooting

a song

for who

in freedom's

air

to hear

Solar Flare

Solar Flare

I am your girder and your welding torch,
  The King you can't approach. I'll pluck your eyes
If, impudent, you dally with my gaze.

I fathered every glimmer of your mind,
  Your fake chiaroscuro, nest of lies,
Those shadows running from my outstretched hand.

Your sunsets, dawns, and bold imaginings
  Don't limit me but mark your boundary line,
The prison where brief sentences are served.

The moon is not companion but a corpse,
  Ripped from your side as you were once from mine,
Though unlike Adam, I'd no need of you.

I can be patient, watch your orbit slow,
  Relentlessly succumb to my embrace,
For one brief second flare, and then be gone.

You're home at last without a place to go,
  Of what you were and wanted not a trace,
The moment that you always ran toward
                              done.

Time's Executioner

I verify the value of blank time,
   An executioner who with one stroke
      Obliterates all trace. Who then prevails?

My death reveals its art yet breaks its rhyme,
   Drives off the spectator who gets the joke,
      And stills the breath that fills its haughty sails.

We boast of our dissimilarity,
   Each struggling to make the other tame,
      One turned to beast of burden, one the yoke,

At odds yet joined in solidarity,
   Our mutual deceit forked tongues of flame,
      The battle hidden in entangled smoke.

The carnage leaves behind a field all dark
Unless your kindling nourishes a spark.

Abraham

You know my name. It's Abraham.
They say I heard the word of God.
But that's so trivial a sign,
The claim would represent a fraud.

You might edge closer to the truth
By holding that I smelled God's breath
Or felt His flesh press next to mine—

Those lyrics, too, would fail my song,
For here half right is wholly wrong.

Not near me. In me. I was Him—
He me: my thoughts, my skin, the hand
That held the knife to Isaac's throat,
This wish that God had granted me
For all the years of earnest prayer
That started with first patriarchs

And threaded upwards through my veins
To reach this distant place of grace—
As if waves climbed each other's back
Until they'd scaled a mountain peak
Which I in one last leap had reached
Or was about to, swelling towards
A sweet release more urgent than—
When my first woman in my arms—
I knew that nothing live or dead
Could halt the rapture's swift approach.

How stop an avalanche mid-course,
A hailstone halfway in the sky,
A thunderbolt, God's righteous force,
The look passed on from eye to eye?

.　　.　　.

Then God betrayed me for a boy,
Threw me from triumph to disgrace,
Bamboozled me of all my joy.

This sacrifice, if you must know the truth,
Was not the overcoming of my ruth,
Nor was it from the first the Lord's design—
But what my faith demanded as a sign.

So now when I cast eyes upon my son,
And then I think of what I might have done,
I know until I die I'll twist in doubt—

Could I have carried the horror out?

Shell Shock

Once upon a time there was a chick
  Trapped inside a shell built way too thick,
Preventing his escape into this world
  Of space and sky and wind and wings unfurled.

Against the thought that he was born for dying,
  He pecked and pecked and pecked and kept on trying,
His desperation made the worse with shame
  For thinking he should be the one to blame.

Perhaps, he thought, I've got too blunt a beak.
  The fault could be my muscles being weak.
Is this a trick that wants a chick more smart?
  Or do I fight with less than all my heart?

The real truth of his failure was quite other,
  His shell a living hell designed to smother—
So that despite his trust in Mother Nature,
  She broke her promise to deliver nurture.

(Unless it was just minerals in the water
  That gave the egg its peck-peck-peck-proof border.
It even could have been a chance mutation
  Had botched the process of poor chick's gestation.)

  Equipped thus with reflection's speculation,
  I flicked the chick my shtick in this oration:

Doomed bird, blind fate says nothing of deserving
  Or any higher purpose that you're serving.
The fact that your condition's terminal
  Is bad enough, don't take it personal.

You're not the center of the world, be humble,
  It's just the way the cookie doesn't crumble.
From my side here, dear chick, I sympathize
  As I, too, peck the shell of others' eyes.

Resistance to the Name

too much breathing
behind these
words

too many dark
nights, dark
days

the words
stop dead

in their tracks

carbonized ghosts
of an incomplete and trivial
hiroshima

under whose unnoticed
dazzle
words become their
shadows

even as we
watch
shielded by that other
shadow
time's compulsive
hand

even as
because we
watch
words become
letters become
blots become
dreams

dreams roaring down
the long night-
mare's back

roaring because
though pain is now
memory
there are no
words

to test the notion of

no listener . . .

erected in minutes
a tombstone
of opaque
text . . .

the buried man
unable to die
without us
whose breathing
topples monuments

is

in this inverted
parable
beyond the shovel's
help
immune to silver
stake

but listen

put aside the study
of anatomy

the heart is
easy to find

in a quiet place

puncture it
with a long
hollow
needle

there's enough
for both of you
and more

dribbled on this
rock
nosing the channels
torn
from earth's aboriginal
core

miraculously arise

words that sing sweet
rage bitter
joy eager
resignation

God Does Not Like People

God does not like people. He's not here for their sake.
    One person at a time is all that He can take.
One person at a time is all that He can love.
    On one branch at a time alights God's milk-white dove.

According to the Book, God fashioned primal man
    To be His trusted friend, as they paced Eden land:
The God chock full of wisdom, boy to understand,
    A duet harmonized—was what Omniscience planned.
But even God can doubt, mistake, and hesitate,
    As when He saw His first begat moping at the gate
And, like all fathers after, needed to acknowledge—
    The best homeschooling ends, and then lad goes to college.
Hence from a rib came Eve
                         to banish bachelor loneliness—

An act, alas, alack,
                that brought blowback
                       to His High Holiness.

For honeymooners nestle in a world apart
    Without a space for others in the jam-packed heart—
Thus leaving poor Jehovah on His own to roam
    The endless corridors of His unrented Home.

Until, as you'd expect, the couple lost their shine,
    And to distract from quarrels, they began to whine—
As lovers do when they're no longer amorous—
    "Where did You go?" and "Why did You abandon us?"

His Son, in future days, would utter that same cry,
    Disturbed by milling swarms of people in his eye,
Since multitudes are not what God set out to make—
    One person at a time is all that He can take.

So when in prayer you gather under dome and steeple,
    God takes a hike and splits from all you pious people.
That's why I think, sometimes, in my most desperate solitude
    I might be in the only state that lets a God intrude.

Bottlepicker Ballad

It's Shakespeare shuffling under moonlight beams,
His gutterals the thunder of our dreams.
Below our darkened windows clattering,
See, there he is, load-bent and staggering.

From brows' deep ledge he looks you in the eye
With force of question mocking your reply.

Hanging Man

Interrogation of a Suicide

From a Spanish question mark
An exclamation hangs.

The chair's rejected ease
Is the point.

Between mark and point,
No-note stutters,

The hole from which the questions pour,
Bounty of the broken piñata.

Under the *signo de interrogación*,
The interrogation of the sign.

"Why?" they ask, and why ask
A question that its answer is?

More strictly parsed,
The answer, it becomes:

Windows boarded shut,
Ears alleys blocked,

Tongue a shriveled leaf,
Gestures stuck to fingertips,

It did the it to be the it
That it is now,

Gain access to authority,
Answer questions not yet posed,

Point in dumb inerrancy
To all our danglings' center . . .

We question the sparrow
As if he'd found an opening,

As if we'd not returned from our vacation
To an empty feeder and a dry bowl.

Alzheimer's

No more the many-mooded sea,
The warm tide swelling in my veins,
Waves battering, then breaking free—
There's only this small drop remains.

No more the diamond-studded crown
That framed my every moment's whim,
I raise no ships nor pull them down,
I've lost the depths where marvels swim—

Content to bleed my content out
And trail as vapor on the breeze,
No whisper of my former shout
To beg time's tardiness with pleas.

Don't pity me, for I bask in delight
Beneath this sun that lights me to my night.

Me, Myself, and I

Me, myself, and I,
    We got into a fix,
The three of us half-sick
    Of one another's tricks.

Me, myself, and I
    Together formed a noose.
How could we shake it loose
    Without some kind of truce?

Me, myself, and I,
    Who never could agree,
Searched for the harmony
    Alone could set us free.

Me, myself, and I,
    In our eternal friction,
Faced up to our addiction
    To singular self-fiction.

Me, myself, and I,
    We've parted our fool ways
And so have cleared the haze
    That hid the bonfire's blaze.

Mood

This is as far as the marble rolls.
The game is done, how tired the sun,
The stars, Swiss movement of the soul—
Though kids in schoolyards have their fun.

This is as far as the bullet goes.
The flesh has done brave duty of resistance
And hangs it like a sprig of mistletoe
Above the heart—but not for mad romances.

This is as far as the lines will go.
If light is ink, then darkness is the blotter.
Our thoughts jam-pack the space where words would grow.
When vessels are precast who needs the potter?

What gives me force to write
                            my tropes on inward hell
Is, with you by my side,
                            I know these moods dispel.

Elliot Alderson

I don't know why I came in here,
  What led me to this room.
Something that I'm looking for?
  The bride, if I'm the groom?

  Or could it be a prison break?
  Can it be my tomb?

My thoughts swirl like the wind,
  They pour on me like rain,
They disappear like memories
  Coursing down the drain.

  Have hours passed, or centuries?
  Am I—or life—insane?

I don't know why I came in here
  And what I left behind
That if I ever found the thing
  Would give me peace of mind.

Can someone blessed
                with courage to be kind
Come end this quest
                and strike me blind?

Six Ways of Looking at a Supermoon

I

The watchman with his lantern light
Astride the corridor of night.
The colors bright of leaves take flight.

II

The moon behind her veils,
A burlesque queen and aging.
How timid is her touch.

III

Moon's silver scattered coins,
Caught by my beggar's fist,
Imprisoned in its shadow.

IV

The mind drills through
The screen of sight
To seize the moon's remoteness.

V

The moon tucks infants in their cribs,
Plucks on the harps of sailing rigs,
And threads the fish's sleepy wandering.

VI

Pearl divers pluck moon's cry
From humdrum waking eye
To where we dreamers lie.

Stranger than Nonfiction

No other creature is so strange.
No other creature has our range,
No other creature sees as far
As other worlds from Palomar.

We never mention in our pride
How sight itself is made to hide,
That almost all of humankind
With parents' help has been struck blind.

We know to mimic, not to be,
We're quick to look, but slow to see.
We've spurned our sense-modality,
Choose thought against reality.

It's only from a distant star
You'd marvel at how smart we are.

Abandoned Chessboard in the Park

Proud of pride, bereft of fear,
Drowned inside the stone
That raised our faces to the air.

They pondered the positions,
The players of the game—
  Tangle of possibilities,
  Mirror of impossibilities—
And found no difference.

Like surgeons who uncover
Too lush a tumor in the flesh,
They sewed up the incision,
Administered the palliatives,
And moved to a more hopeful station.

  Here, under the blind oak
  That holds blank pages to the sun,
  Here, above roots and their hungers,
  No fingers soar like summer lightning overhead,
  No field of forces, bristling thundercloud,
  Urgent and awake.

The news hasn't reached us yet.
The knights are sharpening their lances
For the moment of truth that they won't get,
The soldiers are shining their boots
For all the complicated reasons
They're ordered not to understand.
The royal consorts, still in battle mode,
Have seen the storm between them
Drift away like memories untold.

  "At ease!" the king commands.
    From where two cannon stand,
  The lethal queen averts her eyes.
    The horses, restive, paw the ground.

High drama has withdrawn
  Beyond the circuit of the mind.
No passersby will circle round
  This graveyard where intention lies,
This textbook of the way one lives and dies.

To die

like a dog in the street
    the eyes remembrance stones
quickly placed.

    To straddle the curb
        held tight in the freeze
    of time's stunned flow.

        To point to nothing
            but the moment's leap
        the cordite's progress
                to the bomb.

Freedom

Freedom

Like a bird in a cage we won't know the sky,
Will never stretch our wings, will never fly,

Will praise the wires that safely hold us in
Against the lurking cat's malicious grin

And thank our mistress for her daily haste
To bring our food and take away our waste.

And if a wild relation should barge in
And dare to call security a sin,

Our chirps will call the cat to help us out
And terminate this trumpeter of doubt

So we can bless what we don't know to miss,
Inside the bars that stand guard on our bliss.

Aristocrat

With head held high,
condemned to die,

the proud aristocrat
awaits the blade's éclat.

We, too, will feel
the touch of steel,

and try, head high,
just so to die.

The Blessing

It was when I gave up the struggle
For the storm king's blessing
That the dust at my feet rose to meet me
And anointed me like oil.

It was when the murdered sun
Fell and dragged his bloody robe
That the stab of starlight
Pierced these eyes' accustomed crust.

It was then that the moon's rogue face
Became my father and my friend,
Then that my gestures returned to my hand
Like pigeons homing in from far away.

And then that the storm cloud's distant fist
Broke open like a rose,
Spewing to wild winds the fragrance
Of twice-forgiven memory.

Breath Like Smoke

I

Spanning the shores' fixed
grimace
the dead man leaps
to his life
from white knuckle toil
to white water roil
letting go was the master
stroke

II

Massing at the brink of the
guttural throat
the infant-
ry men
spring
past anxious sentries
forgetting all passwords
except
themselves

Coney Island

I remember when I fought the waves,
How they battered me, dragged me on the stones,
How I broke free and how sweet the air
When I rose to meet it, how I was tossed
And tumbled and fought my way up again,
How my eyes stung from salt, my roaring ears,
How I hardly knew up from down, how suddenly
The whitecaps were below and I could see
As if I watched them from a mountain top
The other swimmers waging their lone wars
Against the ocean's churn and how sorry
For them I felt, how I wished them well
In all their foam-enshrouded narratives.

Some

Some hunt, some hide,
Some here for the ride.

Some get their rush in
The leap into transgression.

The hearts of mice race pit-a-pat;
They hold their breath against the cat.

Some use the fovea to search;
For some the blind spot is their church.

The urge to seek,
Not for the meek.
To find your soul,
Must lose control.

What's past the hill
Can kill.

But how alive
Until.

Amputation

The wolf tears at his splintered leg,
   Held by temptation's grinning jaws.
I, too, for barbarous freedom's sake
   Am driven to self-mutilate
To break the link to love's first laws.

What Good Is Revolution?

What good is revolution
  If you're not liberated from yourself?
What good is evolution
  If set in motion for the breeder's wealth?
What good is loving union
  If your inamorata's won by stealth?
What good these words to brood on
  If turned into a package on your shelf?

So said the rebel
  In silent memorandums to his heart.
So said the devil
  To slyly mock the timorous upstart.

These words appeared
  Upon the unlit tapestry of mind.
And as I feared—
  Since they were true—they couldn't, too, be kind.

Leash on Life

A stray said to a fancy kind of hound
    As they began their sniffy introductions,
"Where can a ritzy leash like yours be found?
    It speaks of class and congruent seductions.

Your collar, too, invokes a world of privilege,
    One tramps like me could only know in fantasy—
So just to talk about it seems like sacrilege.
    Please help me join the club, pal—what's the entrance
      fee?"

"I only have a second," said the hound.
    "The leash's tug will send me on my way.
My mistress, there, she's kind of tightly wound;
    Her schedule affords no time for play.

And sure, she feeds me well, with nice tidbits;
    My bed is warm, protected from the rain;
But all the same, this collar I wear fits
    So tight it cuts the blood flow to the brain.

Worse still, it's not the chokehold on my breath
    That fills the burdened heart with desperation.
What makes my luxury a living death
    Is how each moment of free time is rationed.

I'd love to see us racing hills together—
    To chase the cat and squirrel, fox and hare" . . .
Then suddenly—a snap of leather tether—
    Before the eye could blink . . . he wasn't there.

Bagels Is Brooklyn for Roses

To smell the bagels,
don't need Hegel's
        masterpiece.
Just release
a breath of peace
        after small catastrophes.

Clever Thought

If I didn't have my clever thought,
My brain would be what I was taught.

  If ships don't slip their mooring—
    How boring.

  If thanks to rhyme,
    Ahead of time

I knew the word
    That I must say—

And knew the Who
    To Whom I pray—

Would be a hex.
    Like sex

Without foreplay.

The rising sun
    Turned gray.

The fire that Moses knew
    Turned barbeque.

Because I waited
Till clever thought abated.

Animal Cry

They took away the stars in the sky
They took away our animal cry.

> They'll call a man they hate a beast
> And many kinds of animal,
> Although we know their crimes are least—
> And won't amount to cannibal.

> Those creatures who, bereft of laws,
> Can still be careful with their claws
> And by and large stay innocent
> Without the charge of Testament.

Oh, kill the greed that blights the air
And still the havoc in the ear,
You will take back the stars in the sky,
You will take back your animal cry.

Outlaw

I said that I can't see, and then I saw.
　I shunned the ears' decree, and then I heard.
I held the right to violate the law
　And fled that night the Kingdom of Absurd.

The King himself, he branded me outcast.
　I looked for proof and saw the sky was blue,
The future brokenhearted by the past—
　Which formerly were only things I knew.

And then I found a key—it was my hand.
　I locked the gate—the deadbolt on my side.
I left them to their fate, on sinking land.
　Now with no judge to hate, what cause to hide?

Exempted thus from tax expenditure,
My obligation's but to register.

First You Have to Want to Escape

Tool-using using animal?
Half-blind, groping,

sensing something wrong,
ignorant of fate,
incapable of opening
the stockyard gate?

Cooped in your cage so long—
Awake!

As common as the dirt
and closer than your shirt,
within your reach they wait—
tools of your escape—

the guitar and its six rungs,
the heart that leaps with songs.

Googly Eyes

What eye-play with a baby is,
Should be for us an equal bliss.

My first-year buddies—cute but solo,
Had room for none but Numero Uno.

At two. the guys were cuddly,
But weren't that much into me.

At three, still didn't give a damn,
With their eye-blink attention span.

But I remember us at five.

If only *we* were so alive
And shared that selfsame playful jive!

The Man Who Lost His Shape

For years I lived my life in mimicry.
I envied others for their brilliant shell.
Until a daylight dream's epiphany
Transformed me to a me I knew less well.

Impressions fluttering like butterflies,
Refractions of sunlight between the leaves,
The certainty of nothing but surprise,
Fresh wonders to chase after, not retrieve—

I wanted you to follow my escape,
To join me in my wilderness of change,
But you resisted losing your fixed shape
And shrunk back from my world of wanton strange.

Now I, too, hesitate to plunge ahead.
The magic draws me—it's your loss I dread.

Pride

We don't nix our fear
By fixing a stare
Or running to hide,
But by dint of pride.

Don't quicken our loving
By kneeling and groveling,
We fold love inside
A tried-and-true pride.

For never does hate
A whole life abate
Till after we've cried
And dried eyes with pride.

The ravishing bride
Who's waiting outside
Comes straight to our side
When welcomed by pride.

Il Cielo

Il cielo, il cielo, il cielo,
As painted, say, by Caravaggio.
We waited for the rousty jailbreak blue
To tuck back to its ordinary hue,
And for the cloud, that seemed there for our sake—
The one that pirouettes upon the lake—
To float windborne, a careless child's balloon,
And leave us, as per usual, marooned

   Within our suppositions.

Meanwhile the willow at the corner of the lot
Kept up the show that since then I forgot.
A dangled arm played Johnnie Appleseed
Above the chorus dancers known as weed.
The tall, to city boys, unlabeled tree
Sued us to see and pled its case with dignity.
Invisibly, around and through us streams
Our love, unspoken, like unbroken dreams,

   As if our natural condition.

But now as cares lay leeches on my heart,
The world and I grow radically apart.
Divorce court granted me my best possessions
And left my mate its multiple reflections;
Which in their universe, where all is change,
They toss between them in an endless game—
With touch of sadness, wishing our return,
Soon as we learn it's not a grace we earn.

Awaiting patiently our intuition
That in the aftermath of snake's sedition
Our jealous God has sought and found contrition
And ordered seraphim to grant permission.

A Dog's Dilemma

If you could be less doggy, said the cat,
The two of us would make the purrfect couple.
Be more like poetry and less like fact—
Become more sultry, lithe and subtle.

But don't think I would change your canine essence.
Together we will leap the species hurdle.
(Still you must know that things could be more pleasant
If you would chase the mouse and not the squirrel.)

I'll do my heartfelt best, the hound replied,
True love will overcome my shaggy nature.
I swear my passion's stronger than my pride,
I'll light your sky, and not as Canis Major.

In such a manner did their trembling faith resume,
Though trying to keep love from dying spelled its doom.

As If You Knew

Are you aware your inner voice
Can't quite be said to be your choice?

That those opinions you defend,
Despite all certainty, depend
On something told you by another?
At first your dad and darling mother,
Then friends in places where you need to fit in
And texts where shibboleths are written.

The whisper posing as your self
Is just as likely someone else.
Though you have fought for it with passion,
Your faith's no more than passing fashion.
The fact is that you hardly know
The reasons why your thinking's so.

My best advice is—clear the clutter
And promise that you'll never utter
Support for any point of view
Or make bold claims as if you knew—
And stop repeating what you're taught till
You've spent a year just being thoughtful.

I Paid the Price for Liberty

I paid the price for liberty,
So say I from half-tree high,
Not dangling from a rope
Or squinting through a scope,
But garden-framed with flower scents
From porch-perch purview at my residence.

I paid the price for liberty,
Though others pay a bigger fee,
My tax a touch of blues,
It wouldn't make the news,
But like a pebble in the shoe,
Too small to matter much to you,
The quantity that you can't see
Is plenty bothersome to me.

I paid the price for liberty,
As here I sit in summer's ease,
And lounge beneath a clear blue sky
On my back porch a half-tree high.
And I will have my say
Though others far away
Have better claim
To shout out blame,
Trapped within the fire's yoke
While we, with luck, choke on the smoke.

I paid the price for liberty,
By a tree in the land of the free.
While beating plowshares into swords
We've also dulled the very words
I need to tell you how I feel
About what's false and what is real.

I paid the price for liberty
Here up above the fray so high,
A cappuccino cup held high,
To toast a soldier-son in Tenafly.

The Dolphin and the Lady

Oh dolphin, dear, the lady said,
I've fallen so in love with you,
Elope with me and share my bed,
We'll live our lives *ménage à deux*.

My world is blue, the dolphin said,
It's wet and wild and slippery.
Your dry environs are my dread,
Since levity hates gravity.

Don't worry, hon', the lady said,
You'll never know you crossed the border.
In case you miss your old homestead
I've got the bathtub filled with water.

The dolphin turned, the lady, spurned,
Then leapt to join him from her boat.
But swimming she had never learned,
And ladies, though they dote, don't float.

Attention please—when lovers tease
    don't greet'em
Unless you share the same degrees
    of freedom.

What It Is

My day gig all these years—to help the fearful,
So burdened by their cares, become less careful,
Turn landlocked eyes away from trusted
    landmarks—
Those well-regarded, Hallmark-carded
    benchmarks—

And shift their gaze to stars no hand can reach,
Beyond the anchor-ready white sand beach,
Until they're sailing over roiling water
With no gridlines to mark their place or order—

To stalk horizons endlessly receding,
Ruled by a god who has no ear for pleading,
Their lives at risk to search for nameless lands
Containing treasures no mind understands.

Whatever's found, my touchstone for success
Is guiding shipmates into boundlessness.

When I Said They Are Ugly

It was when I said, "They are ugly,"
That the world swam into view.
It was when I said, "They are worthless,"
That the branch in shy courtship
Offered its fruit.

It was when I stopped trying
To free them from delusion
That they became themselves—
The bars on the window
Of my prison.

It was then I turned my head and saw
That the windowed wall
Was the only wall,
That the bird on the branch
Was nodding to my freedom

As I leapt
Along sights and sounds,
Feelings and thoughts,
Truths that whispered in my ear—
"We can take care of ourselves.

We need no defending
Against the likes of them."

Enemies

On either side of where I stand—an enemy.
Ahead, some *person* raises threat—perpetually.
Meanwhile behind the mind, no less unfriendly—me.

I boast two allies either side to fight this war,
Each one alive with wonder springing from a flaw—
That fount of fool's temerity from which I draw.

I sometimes think that should I triumph in this battle
My enemies and I would share but one death rattle—
Or see the world become a field of standing cattle.

It's not my place to know the nature of the mission
Nor charge deserters for the crime of their sedition.
I know no goal except a fighter's disposition.

I have no strategy except to take both sides.
The conflict never ends and only time abides.

Knowing

Do you know who I am, I asked my mother.
I know quite well, she said: My darling son!
Do you know who I am, I asked my father.
Of course, he answered, more than anyone.

Do you know who I am, I asked my wife.
Much better than yourself, my wife replied,
And then she cut me open with a knife
And catalogued the parts she found inside.

Do *I* know who I am, I asked myself.
I reached to find the answer, how I tried,
But like a package too high on the shelf,
Even standing on my toes the mark was wide.

The question put a wrinkle in my brow,
I grimaced, squinched my eyes and scratched my head,
I thought about it from that day to now,
I took it to my dreams at night in bed.

At last I said, thank God I have no answer.
It's choreography that spoils the dancer.

Moment

The man bore down,
Kicking, punching,
Unsteady in the letups,
As if the boy was antidote

To drunkenness.
Again he lunged,
Black as storm,
Arms lightning strikes.

The boy saw death,
Wondered if it would it be as hard
As terror told him.
He was less with each blow.

The man was everything.
Like eddied leaves, he rose
Into the cyclone,
Torn to nothing,

Torn from the future,
From the man
He would become,
Touching, if he reached out,

Flame and thunder,
And the boy,
Twisting on the grass,
Waiting for rescue,

Waiting still,
Waiting now.

Real Revolution

The truest revolutionary
Is troubled most by ordinary
People—their manner of suppression
Of theirs and others' self-expression.
It doesn't take a tyrant's power
To stifle the emerging flower
That buds from heart through open throat
And wants to send its seeds to float
Through kitchens, living rooms and such—
Then swatted like unwelcome touch.

Fairly
Personal

Little Man, 1941

The picture on the dresser

What are you thinking, little man,
Young as you are with furrowed brow?
Three feet of half-defiant stance,
The war far off, what troubles can you know?

Dear child, what is it puts you out?
What in your inward sight's so wrong?
The parsing of your daddy's shout?
The shadow hanging over mother's song?

And yet you stand so calm and straight,
Your uncontorted face is mild,
Resisting that worst tempter, hate,
Heart caught halfway between a scowl and smile.

I'm proud to stand here as I meet your eye
And say I didn't let your spirit die.

Forest Edge

Wooden throats that sing
Fingers that ruffle the sun's mane
Hands that grip the mother tight
Against the river's endless
Whisper.

Fragment I

God would have the same piano
but he'd play it better.
He'd have your body
but he wouldn't have you fighting him.

A man might cut his throat
much to the surprise
of his closest companions
including himself.

Beneath us the subway train
with its cargo of hearts . . .

Country Drive with Music

We turned the dial and Horowitz was alive,
Riding the Moonlight with his touch,
Touching me as if he were among the living,
Blowing the flame in me to life
From a dark cinder.
He swept the dying notes aside with a dealer's grace,
And then, with clever sleight of hand,
Withdrew a fresh bouquet
From empty air.

Beethoven, too, was with us then,
Horowitz burning with robust life,
While, not to be left behind, mother rose
From her urn at the bottom of the house,
Playing the Moonlight as she used to do,
Solid, poised, swaying on the piano bench,
Touching the keys,
Touching me as I drove
On the country road
Between midsummer boughs
That reached out to me,

Touching me as if they always had
And always will.

Home from the Office

All approaches gone, being completely there . . .
—*Wallace Stevens*

The television's off and I've arrived.
Round and round I went, studying resemblances.
The way a blind man studies darkness.
The way a fallen soldier studies the bullet in his head.
Clicking along the smooth, the featureless rails
of the television express,
the remote my rosary of prayers to oblivion.

Click click, click click,
I forgot my troubles, emptiness, loneliness.
The way a blind man forgets darkness.
The way a fallen soldier forgets the bullet in his head.
I forgot why I should be roaring like a bear,
forgot why you break my heart with your indifferent
fortitude.

On and on I went,
clicking along the rails of that circular journey.
Until I was tired and dizzy with its spiraling.
Until I was ready to exit at the dark and empty station,
walk down the beckoning street
and listen for that briefest gap between my step and the step
of the mugger who all day, I swear, has been stalking me.

A Friend in Colorado

I've always thought, in some part of my mind,
Soon as I caught my breath I'd find the time
To pick up on an interrupted chat
I started with a mountain long years back.

Work brought me there, and time is always rationed.
My schedule refused its invitation.
Nor did life let me make the place my home;
Men, unlike mountains, are obliged to roam.

So now I wonder if a tumbling stone,
Whitewater-driven down a roaring brook,
May be the way a mountain taps its foot.
I won't believe my wish is mine alone.

Black Tide

The words you muttered stripped the kitchen bare—
The faucet's drip, the light bulb's one-eyed stare.
"The X-ray showed some spots," I heard you say,
Voice honed against my memory day by day.

"You're like a slab of meat to them," you said,
After the MRI, further ahead
In what they called your treatment, though we knew
There'd be no stop to what you would be going through.

I think now of your travel there alone
On subways packed with people as unknown,
Almost, as you to me, we to each other,
So unaware of what we've hoped and suffer.

Why didn't we, when we were able, step aside
From that black tide to share the words we held inside?

Baby's Song

The stillness at the center is my mother's arms
Protecting me from pounce of lurking harm.

Her brow is gentle and her touch is soft,
Her grip is strong, she holds me here aloft.

Never will she scold, never will she shout,
Nothing I can do will bring an anxious doubt.

When nightmares startle and I raise a cry
She'll be there for me, certain as the sky.

And when I'm grown and trouble shades my day,
The arms that hold me – never went away.

A White Flag for the General

The General longs for a touch on his crackled skin.
This personage august, this panhandler aristocrat,
Whose massive demeanor admits no equality.

Impatiently, patiently—Generals don't divulge—
He waits for the brush of a feather, the scratch of claws,
Accepts the invidious tokens of pigeon-camp
For careless redemption and gross camaraderie.

For years he pursued them with gestures of welcoming,
Vain chase, imprecation and threat, iridescent shine.
Observers instinctively reeled back in shock, appalled,
Each thinking aloud: "This is not what we meant to mean
If meaning had ever been meant to be meant at all!"

    The pigeons too, nonplussed,
        Refused to trust.
    The General returned to his attitude
        Of invisibility at the given altitude.
    The poetry of his motion slipped away,
        The prosaics of yielding-to-fate held sway.

valediction without memory

imbedded in our grasp,
eluding its extent,
you were the rightful key,
creating secrets your
mere turning would unlock.

The wind that heaves its bulk
against the door could find
no entrance when you stopped
our fist. It rushes in
now, quick as warehouse rats
and scatters far and wide
the traces of your scrawl:

the testimony of
the scuff marks on the floor,
the speech of bric-a-brac,
the brows' rough-written script,
these birthday candles flaring
as you brooded on

the burning of your life.

The Silence

there was nothing to do
but turn the radio on

he didn't punch his wife
didn't yell didn't cry
he turned the radio on
opened the paper
looked for a good war
found none today
but hope was held out

every year
longer than the last
except in memory
the silence was worse
he didn't know why
more and more it left him
with himself
with too much
of too little
with answers
knocked loose from questions
with questions
fluttering in moonless night
with a self like static flickering
on a milky globe
a firefly caught
in the ceiling fixture
of the kitchen where he sat
the Holland Tunnel
at three a.m.
ablaze with unreality
pushing a dead palm
against the river's massive
suffocation

the silence
was not emptiness
not space

a magnifying glass
that trapped him in its bulge
that brought to size and gravity
the insignificance
of insignificant things

the fall of a cigarette ash
to a second death
the disgruntled creak
of the old house frame
and somewhere
between the eardrum
and they say the mind
the metallic jangle
of what must be part
of life

he wanted to talk about it
to invite his friends into the
room
the skin
in which he sat
except that they so banished
silence
he'd forget
forget there was more
to remember
forget there was memory
to forget
forget the silence
coiled like a great
cat
at the edge of a sputtering
fire

until it was late
too late
too quiet
too alone

Lucky Man

I've read Bukowski, Sharon Olds,
The suffering their art enfolds,

    And search my life for relevance.

The scars I carry are so faint
I'll ask the tattoo man to paint

    On those old wounds for evidence.

For certainly, I envy those
Who bear up under brutal blows

Which burrow under each defense
And overturn the vain pretense

    To be beyond our common sorrow.

My road to wisdom takes more time,
The climb up habit's steep incline,

    I'm sure I'll get there by tomorrow.

The Newcomer

The day the TV came, the war ended.
The treaty was signed. Amity was restored.
From an armchair an armistice,
From the tube a truce,
And from a sofa, edges made soft.

In the infinity of the cathode ray,
They sunk their differences,
As people tired of commotion and spats
Will drown a bag of cats or puppies or rats.

We couldn't join them,
Couldn't share in the miracle.
Ruined by seasons and weather,
Spoiled by skates and stickball,
Jaded from running free,
We were immune to their solution.
Their trance gave us the shivers,
As if they'd managed the trick of disappearing
While remaining visible.

When the set clicked on with an explosive snap
And the Cheshire-in-reverse of Howdy Doody's grin
Splashed across our faces
Like yesterday's cold cereal,
It dripped down to the floor
And dropped below monopoly sets and baseball gloves.

We were the last kids in the neighborhood
Who knew each other well,
Comrades in arms against monster boredom,
Never knowing that its square glass prison cell
Was in our living rooms and the battle won.

Mom and dad were the innocents of our world,
Defenseless against the post-atomic radiation
They'd paid top dollar for.
Pulling toward each other on the couch,
They were Hansel and Gretel
Under the stare of an ogre
With the sweaty face of Milton Berle
And the arms akimbo of Ed the creepy Sullivan.
Closer and closer they moved,
An eerie version of sperm and zygote,
Seeking union and self-destruction all at once.

    Finally they touched.
      It was the destination
      That for all the years of their discord
    They had been searching for.

Along the Shore

Are you the wave, tall and cresting?
The low swell's force, seething, wrestling?
The slow scrum's edge, imagining defeat?
The helter-skelter shamed retreat?
Or is your true identity
The fathomless wide sea?

No need to choose, you only need to wait.
Each one of them will one day be your fate.

Discoveries

When I discovered my outside,
What excitement, and what dread!
More than that the world is wide
Or I walk round inside my head.

When I discovered loving,
It scared me half insane
Until I learned of roving
And back and forth I came.

Then I discovered you, my own,
Inside our tortured courtship,
With many a tear, and many a groan,
That heralded my fortune.

Patience

The vagaries of the wind,
   Crosscurrents of the sea,
I ask them how I've sinned
   That they'd take you from me.

Tornados and rip tides,
   They swept you far away
From all the golden times
   When all time was today.

Soon as I thought these words,
   An echo gave reply:
Observe the forest's birds,
   Whose pleasure is the sky.

She'll come to you, if ever,
   When still as any tree,
Without complaint or tether,
   You prove you know she's free.

does it matter

that the sun is bright
that the bay is a dark lacquer
that the tall poles of the parking lot
pin tarmac to memory

does it matter

that the sky's pink haze
opens its iris to infinity
that in their side yards to the left
the trains are as patient as cattle

does it matter

that the broad midafternoon
will never think the night
that ever so indifferently
time pivots the clockwork traffic

does it matter

these colors glints tremors
when you no longer wait
behind this mask
which in your life and in our innocence

was real

Judge Judy's Hardest Case

There are no words to tell you how I feel.
The language of the body is my court
Of last appeal, my formal notary seal.
A written deposition falls far short.

Words of intention are a poor defense,
Tempt lawyered litigants to fabricate.
Your Honor, if I could approach the bench,
You'll find the claimant his best Advocate—

Who in his stance and features, plain as sense,
Attests the vindicating evidence.

Escape from New York

Forgive my walking in your dreams with muddy shoes
And, almost out of fuel, not landing on your cloud.
Forgive my censuring the fashion of your traps
By shunning them, my howling from the hurt aloud,
My banishing the night by burning up your maps,
Reviewing the news from the page of a bruise.

I seemed the pup of expectation, an easy catch—
    Now K-9 comrade of the paratrooper team—
Armed and ready at imagination's hatch
    To leap into the nightmare, liberate the dream.

Borderline

For some time, baby, you looked fine.
Who knew that you were borderline?

Instead of just the two of us,
There's me, you, and Vesuvius.

What was it made our love seem true?
The mirror I held up for you.

I Am This Man

I am this man, so hacked and torn
I have to close my eyes to see
The me I know myself to be.
Survival is my only boast.

The joy once tokened by my touch
Returns as ghostly mockery.
The fires I deftly held at bay—
With strength as certain as my breath—

Now rush like wolves to claim their prey.
I am the gravestone of myself,
Whom wind and time have co-conspired
To scour until illegible.

Yet I've no doubt of my one claim:
These scorns have failed to turn me tame.

Wheatfield with Crows

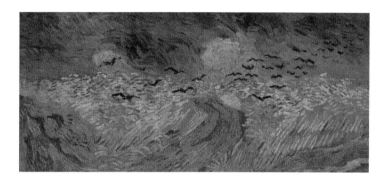

Too late for any medicine to cure us,
  The best thing for us is to never know,
To listen to the voices that assure us
  Contentment shines like gold in hope's faint glow.

Damned devil who dares plant dark seeds of doubt,
  Displacing poppy blooms we farmers grow
To harvest dreams that we can't live without—
  Or wake as bankrupts to the worth we owe . . .

I've tried too long to share my feeble truth,
  That what we reap is never what we sow.
The ugliness of age is born from youth,
  The river drowns us goes on with its flow.

And yet if you could sing my bitter song with me,
The notes would fly like birds above this dark country.

The Dry Field

I scour the stubble fields for one green shoot,
A sign that some old planting's taken root.

And then I think of you, so far away,
Our careless laughter some bright yesterday,

The light we barely knew we walked within,
The shock of parting at the shadow end.

Is this the arid garden that I tend,
The memories that from my life extend?

The Longer Day

With a nod to Reynolds Tobacco

The note reads, "This is life, they say."
Bones buried in unlikely spots
For chewing on a longer day,
A day to which he never got.

    A caravan of *Camels* nabbed the dog
        and every trick,
    And he was chewed for even longer days
        and buried quick.

No more the pup I used to be,
It's my bones buried here and there,
On tables, cabinets, in a chair,
All waiting for the longer day
To chew on what I meant to say.

Not Just Dead

Mom's not just dead, she's extremely dead
   For all except the few of us.
If you never flew the skies inside her head
The once-in-a-lifetime chance has fled
   And no one will rejuvenate her dust.

 Dad was never born for death
   We never thought he'd not be here,
He fought for life from his first breath.
Except for stinkin' cigarettes
   Sparks still would crackle through our air.

Somewhere there's a bridge
   That soon will tumble to the sea
On which these ghosts find passage,
Driven to share their message—
   And you know that bridge is me.

No-Quitter Critter

Against blue sky, a stubborn fly
   In battle with a window pane.
It beat its head so hard that I
   Grew fearful for its battered brain.

I hurried to the little guy
   And raised the sash—but all in vain.
The fly was in no mood to try
   To find another exit lane—

He and the window in a duel,
   To triumph or prove life is cruel—
One lacking mind, one mindless fool,
   Immune to my wry ridicule.

Yet even as I pen these lines,
   I have to hope some god above
Has cleared a way for *me* to find
   As I am battered—seeking love.

Samba for the Dream

The man she loves is not at this address.
He told her but she took it as a joke.
Deceitfully he saved up each caress,
To warm his dreams, so cold if he awoke.

Ah, but who can say
If she'll wake some day
And find this stranger lying in her bed.

What then will she do?
Say his loan is due?
Or else discover who he is instead?

For some, I think, awaking is a dream,
While others dream that they would fall asleep.
One life becomes whatever it could seem,
Another shrinks to less than's worth to keep.

Both are in a trance,
Dreaming their own dance,
A dance where only shadows ever meet.

Different kinds of dreams,
Error versus schemes,
Do opposites subtract or make complete?

Visit to Aunt Sophie's

Why didn't you say this would be
    The end of the world?
Why wasn't I able to see
    The way the carpet curled?

Why wasn't it plain to me
    This was the play's last act?
Why couldn't I hear clearly
    The roaring of the cataract?

The Argument

Along that plain and quiet street a sputter
  Betrays the broken cable overhead.
A shiver of connection—then utter

Black, as if the night had struck light dead.
  So at this moment's cruel repetition—
Again the hope and then the broken thread,

A triumph at the ready till sedition
  Replaces expectation with despair—
What prayer, I ask, would gain what God's permission

To laze beneath a weather calm and fair?
  Oh, I'd accept some rain, one hurricane,
Or two, if when it cleared, love, you were there,

Your shadow at the door on that dark lane
With light behind you—I would not complain.

Terry's Veto of Terra Incognito

"Every single time I hear a Terry Gross interview, I wonder what it would be like for her to do some research on me and do an interview."
— Susan Burton, *The New York Times*

Inquiry rules TV, newsprint, and radio,
Not one celebrity without a staunch pursuer.

But who's inquiring into *me*, I'd like to know,
Don't I deserve a dedicated interviewer?

Catch Terry Gross's genius on the Fresh Air show—
With softest, deftest touch, an inner life's revealed.

Who knew how much of them there was to know?
Who knows how much of me remains concealed?

You think you know me by my look, but looks deceive;
See Terry teach the art of being curious—

Outsiders can be welcomed in, so when they leave
The memories we hold won't be half-spurious.

it's the way they died I remember

the way they fell
the dark shaft down
where listening we lean

the way they flew
brave flag tattering
blindly in this wind

the way they gripped
me grizzled rough
fire of a match burnt down

it's the way they died I remember
when shaftwards down
I call and wait

call and wait

for echoes
mingled hopelessly
speaking lost tongues

Cold Wind

A cold wind whips around the water tower,
Sand taps against the glass at Danny's Grill.
Curbside, a wrist is raised to check the hour,
A flower twists upon a window sill.

Has summer's trace outraced its memory?
How much we took for granted is now fled.
As useless as the boarded factory,
Green dreams that flourished in a foolish head.

Behind the curtain I go puttering,
Tag sale of images out in the street,
Just these two ears to hear my muttering
And empty bleachers watching my defeat.

Yet this I know and proudly testify,
The sparks we struck still make the shadows fly.

The Server's Complaint

This fine-wrought, porcelain cup,
  Finessed with craftsman's care,
Which gently you pick up,
  As light, almost, as air—

Accomplice to the pot
  Aboiling on the grate—
Its substance far more hot
  Than you would tolerate—

Best take it as a work of art
  For your aesthetic reverie:
Since scalding as a lover's heart,
  You sip your tea so hesitantly.

Thus passion, pulsing off the chart,
Is set to cool before you start.

Dreamlife

You dreamt that you were in a dream
But didn't dream that you'd awoken.
You knew the world was not its seem
But not that seamlessness was broken.

Your car careening toward a tree—
You didn't flinch though you could see.
In your cloud-nine placidity,
You thought the windshield was TV.

Some where where you have never traveled,
Perhaps the very spot you're standing,
You'll see the thread where you're unraveled
And find yourself in your unraveling—

To bare a heart past understanding
And wrest yourself from man's commanding.

Don't Make Fun

Don't make fun of me or say I'm absurd.
Though you've torn my tongue out from its root,
The fault is not these feeble, garbled words,
But my unruly need to talk to you.

Cautionary Note

Too often you have followed your own way
   And ended with disaster and regret.
Instead of asking others what they'd say,
   You get them to abet how you forget.

What can they do but look on helplessly
   As confident ambition whispers new
Adventures which you then will restlessly
   Allow yourself full license to pursue.

Meanwhile we see the bridge ahead is down,
   Hydraulic fluid to the brake's been lost—
But you won't tolerate a warning frown;
   You'll keep your cheer no matter what the cost.

We man the ambulance, it's what good friends are for,
So you'll survive another lesson to ignore.

The Late Emergence of Early Speech

If a man were dying
And whispered,
Faint as the seam
Between real and imagined,
Would you,
So high,
Bend an ear,
Squint and struggle to stitch
Patches of early speech?

And since dying is always
What we do,
When you,
So high,
Have heard faint sounds
Of violent struggle
Seething on the shore,
Exposing its pale
Rainbow breath
To the piercing eye,
So high,
Of the tripwire sun,
Where is your shadow

For protection?

In Hospice

The day I found the mess on the wall—

Dumb as a gun loaded for death,
Fighting for mercy from every barbed breath,

Thinking, if thought was still possible:

This wasn't what the singing mother meant,

Rocking me gently through the night,
Promising wrong is always made right,

Pushing me off like Moses on the current . . .

The day I found the mess on the wall—

The petulant toss of a porridge bowl,
The final report from my dad 's beached soul—

Don't know about God or the nurse down the hall,

But *I* heard his call.

Continuation

The dad she's not aware she hates—
    None other than the man she misses.
No matter how much she berates
    You and will not return your kisses,
She'll push you toward his vacant place,
    Where sweet revenge and savage bliss is.

Incognito

Invisible to those most sure they see you,
You're hidden though you have no wish to hide.
And even if you told them, who'd believe you,
That you're there waiting on the other side?

My mother left her fiancé-to-be
The moment he declared, "Oh, Anne, I *know* you!"
"Less my appearance than my mystery,
She said, "is what I would have wished to show you."

The picture isn't in the first brush stroke,
Slow ripening's essential to expose
The self that only patience can evoke,
The secret Who who neither of us knows.

The moral of this is: To be a lover,
You have to read the book well past the cover.

Worry

You worry, you say,
But what exactly is it
You worry about?

Why worry about the car breaking down?
The window that needs fixing.
The bills to be paid.

Worry about all there is to say.
Worry about all there is to know
About me—and me about you—

The endless circulation
Of the names
Our lives are woven from.

Hurry! So little time
For the switch from anonymity
To recognition.

More than house repair,
More than the leaking faucet,
The problem of snow removal,

The impatient queue of illnesses
Outside our door
(Already they wrap around us like vines)

More than shoplifter time
And its piecemeal thefts,
Worry about the stories waiting to be lost,

The stories that hang in our reach
Unharvested
With winter bearing down.

To Ethan, Anxious To Be Grown

When you discover most of what you think you know
    Just isn't so,
Don't worry—knowledge is the stuff of mental clothes
    That you outgrow.

The jumper that you loved so much when you were two
    Would strangle you
If momma hadn't changed it many years ago
    For something new.

Someday you'll scope out grownup peers and wonder why
    So many try
To still fit into toddlers' togs of such scant size—
    Until they die.

Message in a Bottle

In tiniest of places I am lost,
    Too small to find.
Have we been separated or divorced,
    Me and mankind?

If you would take the time to find the entrance
    To where I'm curled,
A life that's shrunk into a prison sentence
    Would be a world.

Seasons

Don't think, my dear, I take it personal
When you unleash your verbal arsenal.
I tolerate the storms, I know the reasons.
The loveliest landscape bows to its seasons.

When heedless winter comes and you emote,
I wear my shouting as an overcoat.
I hold no grudge against your snow and rain:
Here's where I pitched my tent and will remain.

Your globe spins quicker by a thousandfold
Than planet Earth's careen from hot to cold.
Sometimes I take it with a bitter frown,
Sometimes I argue—sometimes just lie down.

But when your sun's warm summer comes my way,
I spread my arms to welcome every ray.

Explanation

Let me explain something.
Of all the injustice poisoning the world,
of all the razor-sharp crimes
that slash the face that wants to smile,
yours is a statistically insignificant sum.
Lighter than a mosquito bite—
Though it rankles the mind.
A mother and daughter stuffed dresses into bags
at the company showroom.
So what?
A marriage was arranged
by counterfeit pregnancy.
Isn't that how history is made?
In high-rise comfort,
with a baby in the crib,
drugs by the hundredweight
were sold.
Surely, the law is more criminal than the crime.
By fraud and deceit
an apartment was stolen
from an elderly couple in need.
Who exactly was hurt
when no one knows the injury?
Millions of throats have been cut
but you're one tooth
on the serrated blade.
A bank check was shoehorn
for a fit into college.
Isn't that the game?
On an island of affluence in a sea of misery,
why not be happier than the swimmers?

More tranquil than a peaceful heart
is impunity.
Why risk the face
when the mask is beautiful?
Even God,
like a deer in the headlights,
doesn't know where the punishing
should begin.
And what is a murdered man
but potting soil for the garden?
If the statute of limitations
is the length of a man's memory,
the past is a cape of fire.
How poorer the dictionary without you.
Where would "sanctimonious" go
or "hypocrisy" find welcome?
Roget's would shudder.
Sections would be purged.
As long as the orchestra plays,
in Auschwitz or Titanic first class
(and isn't the music entrancing)
Why be the first
to stop dancing?

Beloved Enemy

You don't do contrition,
  You wound with impunity.
It's acts of omission
  Accord you immunity.

This written sedition,
  Is my opportunity
To free from its prison
  The pain dealt me brutally.

Cutter

As if from sentence of an ancient god,
No sooner does a wound begin to heal
Than I must pull the knitting wide apart,
Collect the blood to improvise a meal—

Convinced that there could be no greater pain
Than this unblemished body whole again—
No starburst-streaks across cloud-chamber brain,
Held tight anew in history's whole skein,

Without compulsion driving me to grope
The knot where your disaster intervened
And entertain the proven hopeless hope
That we might be in double grip again.

Yet I'd not have your memory so far
As thinnest membrane of a sleep-sown scar.

Bliss in the Abyss

An altar to the romance of the couple,
That fallout shelter pitched against our trouble.

Each side is tasked to keep afloat the other—
As Romeo would find, had they grown older—

Each one the other's water as they swim
Above the jaws of Eden's Seraphim.

Joshua's Tree

My grandson's tree is putting up a fight,
Its foe not too much shade nor touch of blight,

The *casus belli* something more obscure.
Just what it is, can't say I know for sure

Yet can't stop puzzling the mystery
Since this embattled tree marks history—

A shared tableau, a well-remembered scene:
Our Josh, these proud grandparents, slim sapling . . .

           *   *   *

The boy since then is nearly grown a man
While here his tree is stooped, the leaves stained tan,

And yet I like it better than before—
Not charity extended to the poor

But more because of late I've tried to guess
The secret to its pale unhappiness

And have arrived at one particular reason
That fits well with my mood in this late season.\

           *   *   *

Each flower, tree, or blade of grass alive
Has its conditions set to let it thrive.

But seeds are rather light and winds are strong
And nature's best-laid plans can oft go wrong.

Some land on mountainsides in hard clay scrabble
And lack soft loam where roots may freely dabble;

For some the ground's too acid—or too base—
But none, not the most stunted, mourn the waste

Of their bright image of what-might-have-been
And count the need to struggle as a sin.

The fight's their every ounce of energy,
Which, if they thought, they'd think is to be free.

*   *   *

Thus do I praise the bravery I see
When my gaze falls and dwells on Joshua's tree.

Coda

I penned this philosophic meditation
On eve of Joshua's high school graduation
As he leaves home for due assimilation
Into the social fabric of this nation,

The moral plain: to leap into contention,
Rebuff conformity and hail invention,
Speak truth to power, reject polite abstention,
Plus other platitudes I'd like to mention.

Echo

"Unless our love together doesn't end,
It isn't real." How many years ago
Were those Cassandra words so lightly said—
Now trapped forever in thought's ebb and flow.

So many cards the shuffler has dealt
Since we stepped up to play our gambler's game,
Not understanding that the house odds spelt
Near-certainty of loss, remorse, and blame.

In haunted houses, echoes never die,
In backward glances, ghosts renew regret.
No matter how persistently we try,
There's something in us won't let us forget.

Yet since across time's span I still can feel
This pain, false is the claim love wasn't real.

Two Women

She was a woman for whom song came naturally—
Though there is nothing good that can't be taken wrong.
As at first meeting when mom drew the enmity
Of my fair lady, who was asked to sing along

And dance with us as records spun the melody.
The only thing my mother's cheerful urging did
Was freeze her cold as ice inside her dignity,
Then at the curb serve up the meal of spite she'd hid,

Propelled by secret fear transformed into a wish
(For which I'd been dragooned to be her faithful ally—
Why hadn't I just seen her as your basic bitch?)
That by no stretch was any song hers *naturally*!

The fact I didn't dodge her like a gob of spit
Shows even with mom's music I was way too sick.

Fair Weather Friend

I've got a buddy in my head
  Who whispers secrets and wild schemes.
At night he hugs me in my bed
  And paints the colors of my dreams.

We're friends forever, birth to death,
  But he would fade if far and wide
There wasn't fresh air for my breath
  And you, my darling, by my side.

Multitude

The universe observes through many eyes;
A trillion trillion trillion isn't close.
And if one shuts or sleeps or let's say dies,
One petal falling from an infinite rose

Would matter less.
                    Should other great cosmos-es
Be buzzing round us like a swarm of flies,
Perhaps the throbbing, pulsing mass composes
A multifaceted, huge compound eye.

If then my vision lacks the vividness
I'd like, and I can't get to see things clear,
That's not the universal interest.
We're here so through us Something Else can peer.

So much I want to ask, so few the answers.
So limitless the music, few the dancers.

Predicament

Two dogs snarling,
                    afraid to get collateral.
We two smiling,
                    afraid it isn't natural.
The sadness in our eyes
                    can help us realize
Our feelings are compatible.

The Way You Listen

The way you hear me brings the daylight down
To ground. The way I feel you minding me
Will take me up and out, will wipe the smile
From off the clown, undo the blinding frown.

The way my dream of your fierce listening
Was not awoken by a question from
You nor the flinch of your distracted eye
Allowed me to accrue the blue in you,
Drown emptiness with sky I found to fly
On wings for which I'd never known the why.

The way you let imagining replace
Elusive truths whose footprints left no trace,
Erased the need for proof and every
Interrogation of our reverie.

It's Not What You Think

The we who wonder, we won't feel complete
Without a kindred soul to wonder with.
Like storm clouds charged with wind and rain and sleet
We search for mountaintops to thunder with.

Why words at all unless to bind the mind
To brother wonderers on this wide planet?
It's SETI research of another kind,
Our gaze set on the rock that we inhabit.

How did this flowering tree of speech evolve
And give us all these words for thought and feeling?
It's there so you can help my mind evolve
While as one flesh our wounds begin their healing.

Let's talk—yes, even if it's countersense.
Your inspiration makes the difference.

Heart Attack

Arms still powerful, back still strong,
How one small thing can make all wrong!

Imagination keen, flaming with desire,
For something so unseen to snip the wire,

Bring all that was—to have never been—
And cut this striding figure from the scene.

T.

R_{ex}

U_{nder}

M_y

P_{illow}

Trumped

When you know the bus driver is crazy,
  You sit straight, look aware, raise your chin.
Then he speaks but his eyeballs are hazy,
  You smell death and the presence of sin.

When the surgeon who enters the chamber
  Dismembers the nurse by his side,
There's no shame, it's an honest no-brainer,
  If you look for a corner to hide.

Remember the serial killer,
  How he said, hand to heart, he's your friend—
Then chased you from pillar to pillar,
  And you knew you'd be caught in the end?

At rallies, the rungs of each sentence
  Will raise you to Heaven but drop you to Hell.
The problem as always with innocence
  Is how much it bets without seeing the tell.

Cat and Mouse

The clever cat has caught the mouse-oh,
Not one tear shed inside the house-oh.

    The cat has always been mouse hero.

They love his teeth so sharp and white,
They love the way he slinks at night—

    Their love has overcome their fright.

You've put your hero in the White House,
Thanks to his power to incite crowds.

    You do mistake his appetite—mouse.

Comfort Zone

Happy Hour at Charlie's Crab/Palm Beach, June 2, 2017

> *Here's one drink for the Syrians,*
> *One for the refugees,*
> *And one for the experience*
> *Of being none of these.*

How did we earn the right to sit so snug and tight,
Here by the sea, the wife and me, in the eye
Of the hurricane? Where hardly out of sight,
Just one point four miles as the vultures fly,
Hangs ready as a cluster bomb, Trump's thumb
Above the button of the murder cargo—
Poised high to crush a collateral crumb
Of the most beautiful chocolate cake at Mar-a-Lago.

> *Here's one drink for the Syrians,*
> *One for the refugees,*
> *And one for the experience*
> *Of being none of these.*

What the Moon Saw

It was a long walk from the Garden.
We hated to leave, as we hated to grieve,
Since grieving proves the loss and, in fact,
  the losers.

It was a long walk from the Garden.
We hated to leave, and wouldn't leave the
  hating,
But read the Garden in the tea leaves of our
  marrow,
Then drank the tannic straight and tossed the
  leaves in the garbage.

We returned to the Garden, when we found it,
  those that did,
Flame-thrower proud, and burned and mowed
  the damn thing down.

Now we've no sin and out is in,
The snake's a fake, the crown's a clown.

Drone DRAMs Don't Dream

The soldier suffers memory
Infected by PTSD,

Not warned that merely bearing witness
Could undermine the mind's broad fitness.

   Unfazed, the CIA's sleek drone.
   No DRAM program computes "Atone!"

Trump's Trumpeters

... apologies to Mr. Wordsworth

I wandered lonely as a cloud.
My whisper was so faint the crowd
Below could have no way to know
How sky and I made up a show.

Someday I'll be much less alone
As you in your crushed pride atone
For scorning and ignoring me.
Above your heads we'll raise a sea,

Our war-drums lifting startled eyes
To find us in a ruder guise.
Not placid now but great and frightening,
We'll draw our breath and spit out lightning.

Our dervish dancers' spinning shroud
Will change who's lonely as a cloud

The Good Ship

From U.S.S. Morality
We board the bark Impunity,
As captained by Insanity,
First mate a Mr. Vanity,
Their charter a profanity
'Gainst every nationality,
Especially if some frailty
Allows acts of brutality
And fun with bestiality.

The constitutionality
Of rights to wreak calamity
Or just plain old mortality
Are guarded by immunity,
Protected by legality.

Ho! Ho! Come join the levity,
Life, happiness, and liberty,
Aboard Good Ship Impunity.

The Radiologist

He held the x-ray to the window's light.
Suddenly something didn't seem right.

He felt unbalanced and confused
as if the tumor's shadow had worked loose

so that its gross incriminating stain
was oozing from the surface of the pane

or else some horror out there in the world
had lifted evil like a rock and hurled

it with mad vengeance at this quiet room
to join it to metastasizing doom.

I Want a War Just Like the War

Everybody looks the same,
We've given peace a rotten name—

    War's in our blood, no one's to blame.

Everything we touch a bore,
We scour the news for one good war—

    If not for war—God, what's life for?

Each citizen is warring with himself
Or brawling over scattered crumbs of wealth—

    It's war declared or war by stealth.

Inside this bubble where we smother,
We hate ourselves and loathe each other—

    The war is where we find our brother.

So give me good old-fashioned wars
Like daddy fought on foreign shores—

    The war itself as its own cause.

Now all together sin(g):

♪ I want a war, just like the war that buried dear old dad.

    It was a pearl and the only thrill that daddy ever had,
    A good old-fashioned war, like heart's-blood true,
    Where your worst enemy was never you,

  I want a war, just like the war that buried dear old dad. ♫

The King's Defense

The child did say, "The King, he wears no clothes,"
And laughter drove the regal from the town.

    The boy then added, "But I also know
    That you, too, wear no suit, nor you a gown."

    At which the crowd rose up and beat him down
    And begged His Majesty take back the crown.

And when they spoke about it, all pretended
They didn't know the way the story ended.

Watch Out

The Christians kidnapped Jesus from the Jews,
The whites kidnapped the blacks and stole the blues.
Kidnapped Assange, the common man's best sleuth,
Fights hard against the charge he stole the truth.
If you have something special, that's the clue
That there's a plot afoot to kidnap you.

Prophets of the Bible

The prophets of the Bible
  We'd hale to court for libel.
Or better, set their clever wits
  In good careers with benefits,

Expecting that to keep their pension
  They'll put a lid on fierce dissension
So we, without such truths to hear,
  Can speak our lies and feel sincere,

Enjoy a space where we can show
  Our reverence for the long ago
And not have prophets of the Bible
  Upstaged by some more timely rival.

The itch of doubt offends our piousness
As baby's skin abhors psoriasis.

Soldier

Came back from Iraq and the war machine,
Reentered the center of the American dream—
Where manic meets panic and brings forth a child
Whose womb is its tomb as the nightmare gets wild.

Our guilt and our grief, increased past belief,
No saying but praying could help us debrief.
Blood thicker than mortars in midst of the slaughters,
Then calm as a bomb with our sons and our daughters.

Enmeshed in the press of flesh in duress,
Now long for the song of sniper's caress.
At home the soft moan of boredom's revealed
How lies of the hive are slyly concealed.

The burned-out were turned out to make their way home,
Past thunder to wonder why we're so alone.

God Bless the Torturer: A Sonnet

God bless the prison guard and torturer.
Remote drone pilot. ICE enforcerer.
Absorbing rads of anguish and distress
From those whom it's their business to oppress.

They're on the side that goes home every day,
But still they breathe the same air as their prey.
One proud to hold the thick end of the whip,
Both stewing in a toxic mental trip.

So while we focus on the poor downtrodden,
How easily the *torturer's* forgotten.
This priest who urges prisoners confess—
He, too, comes down with post-traumatic stress.

God bless the prison guard, God bless the torturer,
Essential players in the nation's orchestra.

House of Cards

I live in the land of the zombies,
Rub shoulders with the walking dead,
In thrall to laws outlawing solace
Where speech is free since nothing's said.

I'm a stateless Palestinian
Beyond the separation wall.
I'm halfway to oblivion—
Amazing the sniper can see me at all.

In a house of mirrors called manners
Where etiquette's the chiefest art,
If I'm in your schedule planner
I don't have to be in your heart.

I'm angry tonight and I know it.
Don't worry—by light I won't show it.

No Worry

Always copacetic,
Rarely empathetic.
Where, friend, did you get it—
That much anesthetic?

Have you been trying all your life
To stay content and keep it light?
Is every mood and feeling tame
Except inside a video game?

Would you, without a thought, desert
Your friend approaching with his hurt
By saying, "It'll be okay,"
As way of pushing him away?

And do you dare to lift the lid
That tamps the turmoil of the id
To reach the riot deep inside—
The neediness you try to hide . . .

While you make sure your own kid doesn't
Forget the rules and get unbuttoned?
What luck, that feelings you abhor
Can be outsourced to cops and war!

The United States of Armaments

A Ruger mans the living room,
The kitchen cabinet stocks a Glock,
A landmine's doom in daddy's tomb
Can clean the first grave robber's clock.

The new bump-stock AR-15,
The mortar in its carry case,
Outfits a devil twice as mean
As anyone's been in your face.

The full array is here to stay;
I pawned my soul for what I need
To keep the dogs of doubt away
And turn old hurt to hatred's creed.

I lost the knack for play and fun
But none of us will lose a gun.

Dream Residue

We're at war
> when peace can shatter with a word.

All's a bore
> where no one's Ayudar! is heard.

What's it for
> if meaning comes off as absurd?

Who adore
> with each of us both Turk and Kurd?

We the People

Some prisoners had gathered round
To boast of their respective jailers.
The proudest of them never found
That they like all of them were failures.

Columbus said the world was round,
And he was doubted by his sailors.
But if the facts did not astound,
Shroud-makers would have been their tailors.

World leaders of all sorts abound—
Emancipators to enslavers.
Some are elected, some are crowned,
It's up to us to judge their natures.

Marx's Minions

Men interpret
    light as darkness,
Playful purpose
    blithely tarnish.
Who deserves this
    heartless harshness,
Workhorse porpoise
    Said in harness.

New City

Thinking of Assange

We built this city with our fears
From babies' bones and frozen tears

Where snug as hibernating bears
In buildings braced by others' cares

We sleep with closed and open eyes.
(Awakeners are shot as spies.)

Safeguarding our delightedness?
The walls of our shortsightedness.

Citizens

Poor blind, blank wall-encircled citizens
Who seek within the mirror of your reasons
And through the window of your phosphor screens
Your knowledge of this life and what it means—

Who walk the streets inside the best nightmares
That can be had from rising market shares
And look for heroes to combat your fears—
Though'd be hard-pressed to find the peer who cares.

    Poor blind, blank wall-encircled citizens,
    I envy you for your proud innocence.

Under the Lid

The shoe is firm and steady, has the clout
To hide how nervous toes will shift about.

Like posing politicians, lean and stout,
Who won't show slightest glimmer of a doubt.

Your heroes, too, beneath pugnacious snout—
Their brains, like mine, are wriggling sauerkraut.

So if your hope's to be all of a piece,
Wake up, get real, forget that endless tease.

The cry that's throttled in the chest

The cry that's throttled in the chest
Becomes the prisoner oppressed.

The memory we quickly smother
Is what we're doing to each other,

Concealing underneath thick scars
The blowback wounds of foreign wars.

Shock Wave

New-budded leaves are tousled by the wind,
No green thing grieves or struggles to rescind
Adamic sin, or shivers with sharp fright
Against the tempered blade or fall of night . . .

The trembling of the trees has none of these
Presages to the latest news' disaster—
Though toward my kitchen window tsunamis
Arrive in quick succession—faster, faster!

Our trustworthy kaleidoscope is broken,
The world no longer turns to match our hoping.
The laughing sky's diminished to a token.
The smoke from future fires has come a-blowing—

The trees don't know they serve as counterpoint
To show us how the world is out of joint.

Resolution

Easter Sunday 2020

Like throwing matches on a lump of anthracite,
Like dancing polka with the righteously uptight,
Like urging peacefulness, tranquility and calm
As Trump's stub fingers tap the trigger of the bomb—

The only thing that's crazier than craziness
Is placing bets for mankind's future happiness
On our naive belief that words are curative
And make us heroes thanks to careful narrative.

So fuck the butchering with which this world is rife
And leave it to its penchant for unending strife—
For sure as hell I won't be sharpening the knife
That takes the next heart's-blood pulsating, vibrant life.

No Sisyphus, I won't push you to understand.
I'll wait here patiently till you extend your hand.

Outfoxing the News

You boast and bully, browbeat and explain
How noble are your goals, how sanctified—

So bless the bullet in the baby's brain
And patch holes poked in your ballooning pride.

It challenges the best to stay half-sane
When public virtue sides with homicide.

And Home So Far Away

Veterans of foreign wars
huddled in the passageways,
cast like driftwood on our shores,
battle thoughts of better days.

> We pass them by,
> avoid their eye.

> The traffic's rhythm
> enfolds us with them

> as if we share a fate,
> as if we bear their weight,

> > and home so far away.

Out beyond the borough's edge,
streetlights end on graveyard slope.
Ghosts of banished sorrow pledge
help to free our minds from hope.

> Hope weighs you down,
> a leaden crown.

> Here new life grows,
> no undertows.

> This life we're in,
> too much like sin

> > and home so far
> > > and home so far
> > > > and home so far away.

All Kinds of Fun

The Mate's Progress:
A Tragedy in Five Acts

To win at once in love or cards is dull;
The gentleman loves sport, for sport is rare;
He plays the pence of hope to yield
The guineas of despair.

—W.H. Auden, *The Rake's Progress*

I

Forget the notion that from open ocean
    For your mere sake I'll leap into your lake.
No emotional commotion nor love potion
    Will make me make that fatal first mistake.

II

I almost shake to think I'd leave my lake,
    Not fond about your lily-padded pond.
Not even for your sake, though heart may break—
    However you may wave your magic wand.

III

You'll never see me leave my happy pond,
    Swim circles round a frond in your fishbowl,
Not even with the lovingest love bond—
    Encased where there's no space to stretch one's soul.

IV

Yes, kind I am but not the kind of man
    Would leave the shelter of a comfy bowl
To sit inside your fiery frying pan.
    Where I patrol is not in your control.

V

Although it's getting rather hot in here,
    Next date will not take place upon your plate . . .
Debate abated there, the reason clear—
    His waiting mate, her patience waning, ate.

To an Ant, On Waiting Till
She Passes Before Putting My
Feet Up On the Railing

Tip o' th' hat to Rbt. Burns

Ahoy, little ant, can you see me as real?
Do you think that I think, can you feel what I feel?
Or are you too busy running your chores
To ask your what-is-its much less your what-fors?

Ah, little fella, I know your dilemma—
Return empty-handed, they'll be a problemma.
The same thing with us in Sapiens-land;
It's pressing your luck, your hat in your hand,

Impeding the speeding of one in your tribe,
To ask him to wonder how *you* are alive.
For he, like wee ant, is on hyperdrive
To bring an oblation to his mental hive.

How to Give Advice:
Four Rules and a Corollary

First rule:
Don't give advice.

Second rule:
Give your advice
At a suitable distance.
Modern communication allows this
To protect
Chin and eardrum
Depending, of course,
On whether the advice
Is to stranger
Or relation.
Generally, you will not need protection
From friends.
Those you lose.

Corollary to the second rule:
Distance includes, as per above,
Degree of familiarity.
Meaning:
The better the advice
The less acquainted you should be
With the advised
Who should on their side
Never expect to actually
Meet their benefactor
To express their gratitude
And so be exposed

To questions of status
Regarding their being on the
Receiving end
Of advice.
This is why
The best advisors
Are dead.
Witness the Bible.

Third rule:
Don't offend.
Pitch your advice
At other people
People they are not related to
People they dislike
People they exactly
Resemble.

Fourth rule:
Break the first rule only after
Forty years.
Thirty-five for geniuses
Forty-five for the very bright
From thirty-five to forty-five years
Of patiently considering
The advice of those
Who break these rules,
All of them,
And who

Will be numerous.

Sonnet to a Cow

You're way off base if you expect
That noble animal called cow
To view our race with much respect.
They turn their heads, they don't cowtow.

We special? Hear their laughter roar.
They see the way we treat each other.
Their slaughterhouse? Based on our war.
We kill them quick, lifelong we smother.

We're predators, implacable.
But while we only eat cows dead,
Man's an impatient cannibal:
We're eaten alive—starting from the head.

Yes, some there are who show devotion.
For them I'll swim the widest ocean.

Pinpricks

Tiny little pinpricks,
Judiciously applied,
Will cast the bull upon his knees
And crush the lion's pride.

Tiny little pinpricks
Is all it ever takes
To make the strongest heartsick
And give the stomach shakes.

A pinprick here, a pinprick there,
In the street, on the stair,
Whether looking debonair,
Or caught out in your underwear.

Though you think your clever thought,
And boast about your wisdom,
These pinpricks, they have sold and bought
Your central nervous system.

"It happens very little,"
Said woman to the man.
"If ever I was irritable,
It was just a flash in the pan."

"The pan," he cried, "in which I'm fried,
No matter how you mean me well."
Then one more pinprick, and he died,
Ascending to heaven from life in Hell.

William's Syndrome

While with your cheerful voice and heartfelt greeting,
Your earnest eyes, your honest, open face,
Your wish is that each person who you're meeting—
At home, out on the street, near anyplace—
Will know how quickly you can be befriended
For conversations ranging far and wide,
More likely is it you'll be apprehended
As one whose frank regard could skewer pride.

Consider that your understanding nature
Is taken as a clear and present danger.

Here's Looking at You, Kid

There's two totalitarians who rule the land,
Down to secretions of the lachrymose gland.
On guard against rebellion's semaphore,
Each shrug and sigh will be accounted for.

Relax! Release yourself to their control.
It's in their bosom that you'll find your soul.
The apprehensive shifting of your eyes
Exposes your evasions and white lies.

The twisting of the lip, how you perspire,
Is all they need—to know that you conspire
Against your father's law and loving mother,
Who gave you breath and have the right to smother
You in cold blood in your warm bed tonight
Should they suspect your dreams don't seem quite right.

So give a hug, you know we love you, dear.
With that sweet mug, why would you need to fear?

Progress

Since advent of electric light,
Who notices the tilt of night?

And since the marvelous cellphone,
It's hard to know when we're alone.

Likewise we made the atom bomb
But failed to figure our lost calm.

I wonder what we'll next invent
That takes no Luddite to resent.

Comic-Depressive Disorder

Picture a peacock with colorblind hens,
Beethoven riffing with the fellow-deaf,
Say Fred Astaire tap dancing with Mike Pence,
Or Ali rope-a-doping with the ref.

I'm lighting matches in a hurricane.
I threw a riot but nobody came.
Gave sermons to the criminally insane.
Went into the cage but the lion was tame.

I wonder—what did Sisyphus imply
When with a wink he said, *"Arbeit macht frei"*?

Mallard Ballad

I do appreciate the cow's sweet lowing,
The rooster's wake-you-up audacious crowing.
The songbird's silver trill, too, has my vote,
And beaming baby's babbling-brooky note—

Plus moon-trance wolf's hypnotic, long-drawn howl,
And whoooo-are-youuuu interrogating owl.
And yet, if all our sounds were in a sack,
Said duck, I'd take right back my good old quack.

Perfect Empathy

You envy not your friends, the angel said,
Unstintingly forgive your enemy.
With God's permission we have therefore pledged
To grant you one wish from eternity—
Which let us warn you, cannot be reneged . . .
And then the man chose perfect empathy.

The angel gave a look of such dismay,
The man was tempted to withdraw his pick.
On second thought he chose it anyway,
Not knowing that the gift would make him sick.
How could he think that he'd been led astray?
(Was this the good man's fault or Heaven's trick?)

From then on every person whom he met
Induced a stuttering and palsied breakdown.
He'd groan with grief, unable to forget
That each of us awaits a tragic takedown—
As kings themselves are subject to their death
And graveyards are the baby's final playground.

In perfect empathy, the good man saw—
Without the blinders that we others wear—
The future suffering we all ignore . . .
There are perfections that a man should fear
And impositions upon nature's law
That put the strictest limits to our care.

For even blessings should be sought with caution,
And every virtue has its just proportion.

Dragonfly

Why, oh why,
  Dragonfly,
Do you hover
  In the sky?
It's not safer
  Just to fly?

Dragonfly,
  Hardly shy,
Angled by
  To reply:

"Safety's not my real big need,
  Even if what *you* most heed.
I'm a lover,
  Which is why
I will hover
  In the sky,
Hugging pond and reed,
  Checking my airspeed,
Luring rovers over
  To breed."

Orgasm, The Sonnet

Why is it only in a spasm
We gain the gold key to orgasm?
Because, with ecstasy galore,
No rolled-up sleeves, no finished chore.

The Bible's urge to procreate?
We'd not have had our first first date.
We wouldn't question when or why,
Made equal to the damselfly.

In peace at last, we'd recognize
That time is tame and never flies.
In rhythm with the cosmos' breath,
Who would we fear, and what is death?

No longer would there be that chasm
We need to leap to reach orgasm.

Critter Critique

The birds and squirrels all agreed
As they observed us from the trees
That there was something awfully wrong
About the way we sing our song.

I'll trill a tune, the robin said,
But then I'll pause and cock my head
To hear the sound the silence makes—
That darkness our bright dreams awakes.

My chattering, said bushy-tail,
Is not to argue and prevail.
I'll stop and listen to the chorus
Of kindred voices in the forest.

But humans bark without cessation
With never a break for meditation.

I Think It's a Salmon

I forget, is it the salmon or the trout
That suddenly mid-ocean turns about,
Just as the Bible says, and puts away
All modes and implements of childish play
And without hesitation or remorse
Heads bravely toward the archetypal source
With every need and chore and further interest
Posthaste struck off from his or her to-do list.

For countless miles, then, will our hero swim,
Obedient to the primal Maker's whim,
Beyond parameters of gross success,
To find a higher aim than happiness—

Through seas, up rivers, hopefully past claws,
The sole commandment being nature's laws—
Thus scorning all the dangers of the struggle,
Not even asking why it takes the trouble.

And all for what? To transmit life's foundation
To children of a heedless generation.

They'll never know,
                        the headstrong runaways,
Who handed them the map
                        to thread life's maze.

From Brunelleschi to Dizzy Gillespie

In medieval days
When miracles amazed,
The pictures on the wall were flat
And that was that.

It must have been beyond their comprehension
To think a plane admits a third dimension.
And also, since their sensibilities
Were trampled on throughout the centuries

By popes and nobles with their proud éclat—
Like Bible posies, were they, too, pressed flat?
And were they subject to be nearly fainting
By three degrees of freedom in a painting?

The pictures we paint now, no more defective,
Informed by early Renaissance perspective
And struggles of great artists through the years,
Have still not quieted my fears.

Though painting's free to show all planes of space,
How three-dimensional this human race?
Crushed by opinion, ego, stuff like that—
Despite art's progress, aren't *we* still flat?

Coda

This pen draws from a paletteful of worries
About my self-possessed contemporaries.
Though searching like Diogenes, I've found
But precious few can see me in the round.

History of History

We sat around the fire and reminisced—
  As I imagine bygone conjoint bliss.
Then someone wrote the world's first history book—
  Foundations of our social planet shook.

Sweet sharing of our memories outsourced,
  Cruel reign of flag and country gathered force.
We lost the art of trading recollections,
  Lost touch with one another, made concessions

To I-ness and that mightiness His Highness—
Whose cold Law froze the milk of human kindness.

Meat & Co.

I watched a wriggling worm advance
Across the pavement of the street
And wondered why it took the chance
Below uncomprehending feet.

But then the more that I observed
The creature's blind risk-readiness,
The more I saw myself absurd
And felt, well, downright envious.

For isn't every one of us
A trembling tube of tender meat,
Much wiser in its nervousness
Than in its hope of death's defeat?

The worm would have to go to college
To be crushed by such heavy knowledge.

Why Do Roses Smell So Sweet?

Why do roses smell so sweet
When so stinky are our feet?
One brings the bees and sweethearts close,
The other's distanced from the nose.

The first is made for our delight,
The second shod and kept from sight.
It must be that the universe
Knows what to bless and what to curse.

Although the rulebook isn't finished.
(Kids differ on the taste of spinach.)
But still it's true, without the feet,
The rose and girlfriend wouldn't meet.

So what's the moral of the story?
Don't ask too much from allegory.

A Balloon Goes into a Saloon

We're shipwrecked sailors on a desert isle.
  Eyes scrape the far horizon like an itch.
We're would-be lovers desperate for a smile,
  Eyes seeking signs of life—and life's a bitch.

Quiet as a Mouse: The Sonnet

"Pray tell me what you're thinking," asked the cat.
But mouse said nothing from her hiding place.
"Come share your thoughts, I've spread a welcome mat,"
Said cat. "Trust grows when friends talk face-to-face."

No answer rose from mouse's cubbyhole.
The cat, of course, was morally aggrieved—
While to herself mouse said, "Why share my soul
To prove which one of us is self-deceived?"

And so it went between them all day long.
Not even when cat said, "Let's stage a play,
Or sing duets in harmony of song,"
Would mouse be moved to give herself away.

For though the cat can claim good cause to gripe,
Miss mouse is right: A cat reverts to type.

Mr. Turner

After Mike Leigh's movie on the
life of the painter J.M.W. Turner.

Mr. Turner's servant woman,
He fucked her like she wasn't human,
His only sound a gruntish cry
Between twin zippings of his fly.

You hardly need to be a prig
To call the man a filthy pig,
The single mistress of his heart
His dedication to his art.

Obnoxious Mr. Turner, so obsessed
His palette lacked the love to mix with sex.

Soon as you think you've got the measure
Of William Turner's ugly pleasure,
He trills with song like bird on bough,
Purrs softer than the cat's meow—

The day an ordinary frau
Ignores his you and sees his thou
And listens to his conversation
With rapt, unstudied concentration.

The proof that on his palette he can mix
The varied tints and shades that color sex.

Snugsville

Good sense says it's verboten
To criticize those chosen
By marriage or by birth
To be your Central Earth.

To question their odd ways
Could crack that fragile vase,
The hard-won harmony
That lets caged birds feel free.

Just ask the snake. He knows
The law of being close:
Since poison sacs will fill,
Find targets past the sill.

Turn private petulance
To foreign virulence.
No blowback when you kill
The stranger past the hill.

But on the other hand,
Snake said, and checked his gland,
Exceedingly be careful
Of who you give an earful.

Domestic criticism
Or even witticism,
Inspired to break ennui,
Could mean the joke's on thee.

If You Want to Be a Pirate

The reason pirates wear a patch
  Is not because that eye is blind.
When they climb down below the hatch
  The dark-adapted eye can find

An item that they lack—or knife—
  Held throat-high by a hidden foe.
So *I* keep ignorance alive;
  How learn, if all I do is know?

If more of us would feel the same,
The air would be less thick with blame.

Honest Lion

The lion said to Androcles,
   Your help has given pain surcease.
Take my advice, get off your knees
   And race to far antipodes.

Though you're the greatest CNA,
   You haven't changed the DNA
That mediates the way I slay—
   And I haven't had a bite all day!

Zoo Story

The lion, tiger, toucan, too,
Are envious of me and you,
With roars and screeches shout their rage
That humans got the bigger cage.

Mean Man

I'm a mean man, mean and sour,
Could watch somethin' dying for an hour.
Can't stand singing for a minute,
'Specially with love and that junk in it.

> I'm mean,
> I'm bad,
> Knock you down
> Before I'm mad,
> I'm mean.

I'm mean and evil and the devil's my man,
My future's a fire, my past is the fan,
I've known lots of people but they're down the drain,
Never much liked 'em, so I can't complain.

> I'm mean,
> I'm bad,
> I may get angry,
> I'm never sad,
> I'm mean.

I may be a bottle in a bottle in a bottle
But the last one'll knock out your eye.
I never lose my grip, you can smile if that's your trip
But I'll keep hold of mine till I die.

> I'm mean,
> It's my thing,
> Dogs'll howl
> Though birds may sing.
> I'm mean.

A woman's nothing but a sponge and a leech
'Less she gets to places that I can't reach,
And the minute she leaves off-a her chore
Is the minute I throw her out the door.

I'm mean
At my best
And my worst
You're too good to guess.
I'm mean.

I walk into a bar where people don't know me,
I don't say nothin', like it's all below me,
I don't know why the women jump on my bus,
Guess they're waitin' around to hear me cuss.

I'm mean,
They love it,
If they don't
They can shove it.
I'm mean.

I left my wife on the honeymoon,
Very first night, but none too soon.
When I told her I wanted to see her naked
She took off her clothes but she did not shake it.

I'm mean,
I know it,
Feel good,
Don't show it.
I'm mean.

Most of my women, I just throw 'em down,
Rip off their clothes and go to town.
I ram right through like an express train,
Don't start having fun till they start to complain.

I'm mean,
I'm bad,
If I'm not enough for you
You can meet my dad.
I'm mean.

Diatribes

Congratulations!

Uncle Walter never snuck
Into your room to fuck.
You grew up in the glare of hope,
Misunderstandings weren't settled with a hammer or a rope.
Your smile as passport, you were able
To cross the border to the cool kids' table.
You aviated over every hurdle,
The milk of human kindness didn't curdle.
You didn't skulk at the back of the class
Like an ass,
Suitably suited and degreed,
Your university wasn't the street,
The people who raised you
Didn't disgrace you,
No one lost their job or worked too many hours,
On birthdays and other fine occasions there were flowers.
You learned your grammar and your history,
And if the hardships of this world remain a mystery,
The God of your invention
Who puts the bad boys in detention
Says we all get our deserving,
Including every prisoner and the term he's serving.
No wonder you've grown confident, if not content,
Blinded by good fortune to the way the rules are bent.
If the car breaks down there's plastic for another,
Or else you borrow from your dad or mother,
And will not lose the job and miss the mortgage payment,
You'll keep your silverware, your holidays and fine raiment,
Pleased that from your up you can look down
To give the deadbeats a smug, reproachful frown,

Armed with an explanation that to all your friends rings
true—
    That the holy mess their life's in
    Is in the way of a confession
That they're not as good as you.

Insouciance

They float within a languid trance
Of cavalier insouciance.

Quick-witted sophistry
Defends their apathy.
Lost in a blur of sly evasions,
They keep cool hold of their complacence.

Their vanity's inanity
And wan incuriosity
Can only reference
A bland indifference:

An endless dance
Of nonchalance,
To dip and turn
In unconcern.

Ever indisturbable,
Always imperturbable,
The smug and guiltless innocence
Of their serene insouciance.

Savage Myth

The myth of the savage
Helped us to ravage,
Boil nations like cabbage
And label the damage
The *sin* of the savage.

For what is savageness
Except the baby uncaressed?
The parts your parents didn't bless
Have left your brain in such a mess,
Chock full of misplaced guiltiness,

You need to murder to confess.

Behind the Wall

It's so snug and safe in here,
Buttoned up against our fear.
Never need to shed a tear,
Suffer doubt, or give a care
For another anywhere
Past this haven of good cheer.

Everyone outside our wall
Hardly matters. (Not at all!)
Should they rise, we'll make them fall,
They've no right to stand up tall.
If they try, we're set to haul
Scoundrels into court to crawl.

Should they choose to scream and shout,
Organize and mill about,
Bold enough to try and flout
Laws we make from our redoubt—
Passed to us, the Lord's devout—

Maybe we'll just wipe them out.

Scary Movie

What I wait for
They already know.

They can't hide it.
It shows in their eyes.

I carry it for them.
Unspoken.

Dread. Like a package in a bus
That will explode. . . .

Bad things happen to good people.
It's what movies are about.

Good people all.
The worst often better than the best,

Seen with a child's first
Unflinching gaze.

They bear it patiently.
With perfect trust.

I know something will happen.
I can't help them.

Can't ward off the blow, the gunshot wound,
The tragic loss, the realization.

We are all relieved
When it happens.

The worst is over.
We didn't know them well.

Our lovers are alongside,
Our familiars safely nestled.

We will go home
Talking like people
Who have left fate behind them.

The Human Race

With every step I hit a human face,
And proudly, since there's no cause for disgrace,

Say, "Sorry, but you'd do it in my place.
That's why we call ourselves the human race."

The Therapist's Complaint

You go to the store to pick out your clothes,
There's only one size (they alter your bones),
The clerk's voice is flat without semitones,

    You notice your wishes have been presupposed.

At home they untune babe's lullaby croon
And cookie-cut lovers' changeable moon,
Dragooning us into a comic cartoon

    As drawn by those goons, the techno-platoon.

My own specialty, professionally,
A kind of free-style psychotherapy,
Which I can't describe for the life of me.

    It happens to two simultaneously

As words bubble up spontaneously.
You'd see what I mean immediately
If really we lived in the Land of the Free.

Everybody Wants

Everybody's eager to be recognized,
Everybody dreams of wide renown,
Everybody's anxious to be maximized,
Everybody hankers to hear praises sown.

    Everybody wants a crown—to rent if not to own.

For this high aim, stained histories are sanitized.
We certify that secrets stay unknown
So pompous posers won't be satirized,
Their names pronounced in less than reverential tone.

    The king wants seat belts fastened to his throne.

Holy Nation

The qualities we hold most sacred
Are hilts to daggers of our hatred.
Without our God and Holy Nation,
We wouldn't have the wars we're waging.

The White Semite

After viewing the James Baldwin documentary, "I Am Not Your Negro"

This poem levels no argument against a country or a people. What it stands in opposition to is bigotry—especially the reverse form of it that shields a group from criticism. What you see below is a light-verse reaction to our failure to remember the lessons of history and put ourselves in others' shoes—which are the same shoes that all peoples have worn at some time, in their own encounters with brutal oppression and grievous suffering.

Q: Why are we Semites tight with Whites
When from pogroms and such delights
Without compunction we were tossed
To feed flames of the Holocaust?

When Jews believe they are—were always—White,
Invited to the club where might makes right,
And when they spurn the image of the meek
For *their* good turn at pillaging the weak—

Assisting Whitey's worldwide wild mayhem
To do to others what was done to them,
They fantasize they can evade
Blood libel White Supremists on them laid—

As if their graves won't hide inside the smoke
Since they're the ones the blazing fires stoke.
Kill Arabs? Whitey doesn't raise a fuss.
"Good job! Congrats, my boy, you're one of us!"

We Jews who still resist participating?
The news is that we're every one self-hating.

Dr. Ulysses

All day I reconnoiter
The intricacies of speech.
Sometimes I idly loiter,
Sometimes I run top speed—

Then freedom's lease expired, return
To kingdom of the amateur
With subjects less inspired to learn—

Their heads cocksure,
Their fingers fumbling,
Like babes who know what blocks are for
But can't keep them from tumbling.

Aiee, aiee, poor me, poor me,
God help me if I say I see.
The diatribe-tribe would murder me.

Gremlins

Do you have gremlins prowling in your head,
Those Pac-Men of a teeming mental space
That chomp upon your thoughts till they're slam dead
While sparing your strong body and fair face?

Do you have gremlins prowling in your head
And turning your neuronal wilds to waste?
Do you depend on what you've heard or read
And then pretend that you've got things to say?

There's hope, my friend, the docs have found a cure
That can restore the lushness of your mind.
The trick is trying not to be so sure
And always, with another, to be kind—

And though the ground is hard, the way is long, the trail is
    cold,
To extricate and silver-stake the lies that you were told.

Collapse

So what's it like to live atop a bubble,
    Relaxed and carefree, not a thought of trouble,
Till suddenly you're standing in the rubble
    And asking scientists at NASA's Hubble
To search for distant worlds more habitubble?

Pyramids

The pyramid was built to tower tall
  So shadowed men would feel their power small
And egos, gazing up, would go freefall,
  Revolt reduced to ping-pong wrecking ball.

Old Pharaoh would wax envy if he saw
  How modern states crush citizens with awe.
Could *we* plot movies, write the dialogues?
  Composers, dancers—they must be as gods—

While you and I trudge heavily kerplunk,
  Assuming it's our sorry lot to be,
  Inside this manufactured harmony,
Effectively, creatively, defunct.

Handful of Gimme,
Mouthful of Much Obliged

I'll call you back, they always say,
    I'll call you back, I'll call you back.
They set the bomb fuse on delay
    And leave before you feel the thwack.

They never shun a helping hand,
    Thanks offered like a platitude,
Repayment, they don't understand,
    As per their short-lived gratitude.

Complain and they will banish you,
    They'll cross you off their invite list.
They'll airbrush and they'll vanish you—
    Till next you're needed to assist.

The only thing they do for you
    Is after you've been overkind,
Regain the power of rebuke
    And give the posers a piece of your mind!

Culture Wars

The caterpillar jealous of his freedom
Defines confining chrysalis as prison.
So does smug grub snub claim to airy kingdom
To creep and crawl forever in his tedium.

Then there are others standing tall above him
Who say a mask subtracts from liberty.
They'll win the prize named after Mr. Darwin
To die both of the virus and their vanity.

Arrowheads

Does baby ponder over time unborn?
  Do lovers reminisce on loneliness?
When casting votes, do we recall the scorn
  We leveled at last savior's phoniness?

We live in forward motion, straight ahead,
  Ignoring ample reasons for self-doubt.
Momentum's our slave-driver till we're dead
  And handed to church eulogists
                                    to figure out.

Altered States of Addiction

Welcome to the as-if world of passive addicts.
No one anywhere, I swear, is quite as sad as
Those who smile the while they look you in the eye
As if it's you—not booze—that gets them high.

   Mustn't give a hint of what one knows—
   Even if it shows like toper's nose.

Their mental osteoporosis makes
                        the tactful agile
To shield them from a more objective take—
                       they *are* so fragile!

Braveheart

You hide from your timidity
  So nimbly and so cleverly,
It's led you to your certainty
  Of self-worth and security.

The friends you gather by your side
  Are pledged to shield you till you die
From doubts that might cave in your pride
  By riding shotgun for each lie.

Oration Nation

In the beginning was the Word,
And was God ever full of It!
If you dared call His Word absurd
He'd damn you for the Hell of it.

His Word bred other words like rabbits—
And have we had our fill of it!
Talk has to be the worst of habits—
But everyone's permitted it.

We'd rather talk than eat or breathe.
Talk holds us in benumbed submission,
Imprisons us and takes the keys,
Invades our ears without permission.

Beat down by words with no escape,
It's not far-fetched to call it rape.

Because it is

> "In the desert
> I saw a creature, naked, bestial,
> Who, squatting upon the ground,
> Held his heart in his hands,
> And ate of it.
> I said, "Is it good, friend?"
> "It is bitter—bitter," he answered;
>
> "But I like it
> "Because it is bitter,
> "And because it is my heart."

—Stephen Crane

Nightwalker

Calming oceans in your bones,
Leaving less than the wind,
I walked with you.

Crossing the western rim,
Walking backwards from your life,
I sheltered you.

Ghosts walk not in the sun,
Their shadow arms
Won't reach to you.

At night the clock clears its throat.
A star's long walk
Is closer than you.

While thoughts as black
As the track on this page
Still fly to you.

By Your Side *(song with musical notation)*

You laugh,   *(E,B)*
      I'm there   *(G,D)*
You cry   *(E,B)*
      I'm there   *(E,B)*
Close to you,   *(G,D)*
      I'm close to you . . .   *(E,B)*
Though others say   *(E,F#,E,F#)*
      I'm far away   *(D, B,A,B)*
            I'm near you,   *(F#,B,B)*
Near or far   *(D,C,D)*
      I am by   *(C,Bb,C)*
           Your side   *(Bb,A)*
No matter where you . . .   *(B,A,G,A,B)* . .
Are you
      Laughing?
Are you
      Crying?
There I am.
Are you
      Waking?
Are you
      Sleeping?
There I am
      There I am.
Just look and see
      How the light
           Is falling
How sounds that fly
      Through the night
           Are calling
Wherever you may…
      Be calm
           Be bright
When you go
      To sleep tonight
           I'm near you
I am by your side.

Identity

Void's edge pulled taut will clip the fingerprint.
Childe Arrowe, early scholar, plods to war.

No breath so dear but we won't let it go.
No word that isn't tattered by the light.

Each day for thirty years your burdened name
Was haloed with the dust that dreams dispel.

Two blind-men's canes, these eyes advance upon
Cat-whiskered darkness, tapping true from false.

Innocent, the storm-downed transmission line.
Bloodhound too hungry for the careful work.

And Laius, too, was searching: for his son,
As for a garden guarded by a snake.

Kidnap!

And then the harsh commander barreled down
And hurled you to the shadows with her frown

Where back and forth you paced within a cage
Set firm and charged with wires of ready rage.

No Orpheus I, you no Eurydice,
Kept at a distance I could feel, not see—

The crushing weight, the theft of loyalty
That forced you to renounce all thought of me . . .

When was the moment of your first outcry?
Did you call out for me? Has longing died?

Was it the impulse of a second's blink,
Or agonizing months to slowly think:

   Where are you dad, why did you go away?
   What secret does my mother's scorn betray?

   The time when he returned, half stranger then,
   And momma screamed and said he was no man

   Since he refused to answer her attack,
   Respond in equal fury, give it back . . .

   The elevator ride, I held her sleeve,
   Mom shouting to the doorman, "Should you see

   This man again, you will not let him in . . ."

Your shock, your shame, a child's confused chagrin,

The palace of your nightmare made it seem
That lo! the King is dead, long live the Queen!

Understanding How Assets
Can Be Divided in a Divorce
But Having a Hard Time
Not Getting Bitter about It

Help me solve a tough enigma:
When did daddy lose charisma?

There's some of us would think it sad
To not look up to one's own dad,

Might think it haughty arrogance
To have no use for his old man's

Companionship or common sense,
To spurn the hand that he extends.

They couldn't hope to know the pride
Of one without such urge inside—

To be a man so self-created,
He wants no vote to stay top-rated

And casts his jaundiced eye of scorn
On those who need a father to be born.

How'd he resist paternal seduction?
Through juvenile maternal abduction.

When mother threatened love-removal,
He shaped his mind to her approval.

Forgetting Remembering

He cringes backward from my touch
as if I would reveal the stump
of disremembered mutilation.

Here, I tell him, hand to heart, here
is where you find the missing part.
He drowns my words in innocence.

But I remember much too well:
The date, the place, the pain of it.
No memory needed for the wound.

The blood, I won't allow to dry,
I'll tap the bleeding till I die
to keep my pen in fresh supply.

Indifference and Hope

Whatever love I might have asked of you
You gave good riddance to some years ago.
Though foolishly I claim your debt is due
And strain each day to reap what doesn't grow.

Your blank indifference blinds you to my grief—
How tear the blindness from a sighted eye?
Removing faith from mine might give relief
By letting my eye see I shouldn't try.

We stand athwart a single telescope.
My side expands, yours shrinks me to thin air.
My compound glass binds memory to hope
While your objective lens is my despair.

And yet I only ask you to recall
The days my very nothing was your all.

The Waiting Game

The limit of a conversation
Is either party's termination.

This muffled clock's relentless as the setting sun.
An actuary would advise me to be blunt.

Your own process will take much longer to unfold,
Affording time for wisdom as you, too, grow old,

Until you think to ask, informed by riper years,
The speculative questions held in long arrears.

And then, as if by instinct, when you turn to me,
An absence will confront your curiosity.

So while the blood cells march to drumbeats in our veins,
Forget what we have lost, make use of what remains,

Forgive, as well, this bid to open up your eyes
And credit my intent to bring us side by side.

My words are not about who will have won,
    But warning sent—before we're overtaken—
    To one whom through it all I've not forsaken,
My proud, disdainful, disaffected son.

Imaginary Garden

From this broad barren field of dust,
Beneath the stare of ancient skies,
Rejecting reason, slave to trust,
Envision here a garden's rise.

What is a seed without an earth?
What seed is satisfied intact?
What child's content before childbirth?
Who's not unborn till his last act?

Each side is groping toward the other.
I couldn't tell you which is which.
Strange how if not embraced they smother.
What caterpillar knows its wish?

Fate's prey, I'll stand my vigil on this plain
Until your stubborn fist lets go its grain.

hearthold/hearthhold/earthhold
gravity and its discontents

I

No matter how you lean
    And turn and twist about,
Your painful origin
    Gives chase and finds you out.

Sir Newton was amazed
    How earth maintains its grip
Invisibly with stays
    From which no thing can slip.

So too that motley crew,
    The few you call your kin,
Who happenstance engendered you
    And hold you tight—
        though might you fight—
            as skin.

II

A strange attractive force!
    The more you think you roam,
Your curving comet's course
    Deposits you at home:

The unremembered shame,
    The prison guards called dad
And mom, who made you tame
    As angels, guilty-sad,

Till eagerly you fled
    Into your sky's today,
Convinced the past is dead—
    Still starring in
        the original sin
            Of the original play.

Prodigal Father

My son, you pretty much have spent your life
In truckling first to mother, then to wife.
"But no, I fight against them," you would say.
Dogs fight the leash, but mistress gets her way.

Of course, you're sure my hidden interest
Is not your welfare but my bitterness.
Now *I* deny the claim. Dad moves too fast
For that old snake to snag him in its grasp.

I reprimand, but also I beseech—
So is hope's butterfly, though out of reach,
Never out of sight. And though you scorn
My warrant, it's been fixed since you were born.

Theirs was the job to brainwash, mold, and train you.
Your father's role? To show how chains constrain you.

Five Fathers

Two fathers had they, mother none.
Thus sense, not sensibility.
My four grandkids, my precious son—
Need Nation for stability.

Two macho mothers, had they, loved and feared,
Who filled their innards with themselves,
Their souls in limbo left uncared.
The wounds show through but no one tells.

Their own lives, had they, never grew
Beyond the daddymommas' reach.
You might say that they never moved,
Though zipcodes separate had they each.

Two fathers had they, mother none,
Which leaves a father with no one.

There Is a Time

There is a time when everything you haven't said
Eclipses anything you still may have to say.
So long ago, it seems, I put my hopes to bed,
Now live what might have been in dreams that flee the day.

There is a time when everything you haven't said
Is fifty feet of water pressing on my chest
Until with steady strokes I choose the air instead
And sunlight proves which one of us is cursed, which
    blessed.

There is a time when everything you haven't said
Turns into headlines spooling from the evening news,
Announcing all the ways the world is being bled,
Inspiring heirs of Bessie Smith to sing the blues.

There comes a time when everything you haven't said
Draws boundary lines between the living and the dead.

Fiftieth

Make this the year of your dissatisfaction.
Without a fight, no child has ever grown.
Let torment come to rouse you into action
In exile from your cozy comfort zone.

I'd like to see the might you showed the world,
That brilliant night when your quick flame was born,
Deploy upon the field where you were hurled
To war against this blight of hate and scorn.

The ear of early memory still resounds
From where you touched my life with your first cry—
No caution to the nurses in their rounds
Who rushed you from your eager parents' side.

My mind has need to keep this scene alive
In hope that you will see your purpose thrive.

Lighthouse Dreams

Perhaps it was with humor, it could have been despair—
But soon as I awoke, this thought crept to my ear:
When you've become as aged, you'll remember me
The way a lighthouse keeper dreaming hears the sea.

I'll be the waves that cast their bulk against the shore—
Five thousand miles of gathered force that hurtle toward
A destiny they search for—locked behind your door—
That shield against embrace, mistaken for a sword.

Sometimes in sunlit merriment—sometimes in storm—
Or hope—or desperation—another effort's born.
Of all the different dramas, each one ends the same—
An army routed in a riot—of shame and blame.

That night the whisper came again and said to me:
The lighthouse keeper's pride is bulwark to the sea.

Splinter

I have a splinter wedged beneath the skin.
Again, again, again, I feel the sting.
With fire-blackened needle I'll begin
To draw it out as preachers would do sin.

Practitioners of medicine advise
To start the job before the flesh infects.
I'm proof that fools don't listen to the wise;
The heart resists what common sense directs.

Myself and splinter play our tug-of-war,
But splinter's been an able enemy,
With roots that pull against my gathered force,
Engrafted, as they are, to memory.

Yet I won't let these second thoughts disarm me,
I'll dig you out no matter how you harm me.

In Conclusion

I, having mourned your distance half my life—
Who welcome suffering as love's fair price—
Will leave the field to your imagined strife.
You need not grieve, my labor will suffice.

The day you join my sister, friends, and wife
Around the expectation of a grave,
Will their lamenting cut you like a knife
Or will you keep to hibernation's cave?

And will your safe resentment still so nice-
-ly fend me off with heat-shield insulation—
The pain of loss, as always, numbed by ice
And shrinking from the sun of my affection?

Since all my beckoning could not entice
You, will my absence offer apt advice?

Poems per se

The Poet At Home

The boss bursts through the door:
"You waster! Out from there!"
I drop down to the floor.
He pulls me by the hair.

I fiddle while the money burns; I know he's right.
Beyond the window, stretching past the reach of sight,
A prisonscape of blue-light rooms outstaring night
Is ambered in a silence that the truck, the gun,
Can't break to ease this tyranny of work and fun.

The Art of the Triple Play

Before the ink dries,
The echo dies,
The baby cries . . .

Before loneliness has lost its sweet
Taste, and caterpillar greed
Has made green silence bleed . . .

Before the hand pounces on the remote,
And naked winter has grabbed his coat,
The drowner is rescued by boat . . .

Before too little is too much,
The trap that we call freedom shuts,
We're caught in our own sweaty clutch . . .

Before all that
Is turned old hat,
Sat on and flat . . .

What did I mean to say?
Cat slipped away.
Back another day.

Blue Sunday, Blue Monday

Catching Blues with Dave and Mike on the Sound

Blue they call him, but he's silver on the line
    And steady as a bulldog on a rope.
Quicksilver as he dangles – then he's mine.

He gives the boards a drumbeat of surprise,
    Astonishment replacing early hope
Within the tarnished silver of his eyes.

Come morning an alarm clock's silver gaffe
    Pulls me up thrashing from sea dreams to grope
My way back to the office, and this craft.

Ticket for Tiresias

Fire! Fire! I shouted to the theater crowd.
    "Hey, quit the chatter there! Shut up!" they cried.
"You're ruining the show, man, settle down!"
    It seemed I could have screamed until we fried.

What then to do but jump up on the stage
    And there announce the coming conflagration.
You'll never guess what happened next—so strange!
    The crowd yelled bravo for my "fine oration."

The more I urged them to outrace the flames,
    The more my words were scanned as shapes of art.
I told them No! I wasn't playing games—
    And still they lauded how I spoke my part.

At last I said, I can't destroy you, Tragedy,
But I will sure enjoy you, Comedy!

Hidden Agenda

The poem doesn't say I'm smarter,
It's there as conversation starter.

It's not a tenet of belief,
But thoughts that I would like to weave

Into a friendly back-and-forth
To find out better what they're worth.

The talking's what the poem earns;
A page warms only as it burns.

While through our mutual investigations,
The bond we forge outlasts the whim of nations.

The Sad Lexicographer's Approach

A poem
Is the hand the severed hand rejoins
Is the deck reshuffled for an honest game
Is the locomotive's hoot revealing night
Is love proved real with noises from the street
Is the shopper on line for a meager shelf
Is the hollow reed to the amber's bourn
Is the giant's squint between plucked notes
Is the infant looking at his hand
Is the clanger on the bell
Is the bane of camouflage
Is the pilot's sketch for the landing strip
Is the breath that spreads the newborn's lungs
Is the rich man's toy, the poor man's gun
Is the first thing thought and the last thing said
Is the pinprick reminder of sleep's magnificence
Is the stranger's calling card to himself
Is the mouth's invention of the ear
Is the surprises lies produce
Is the grownup's gibberish, the child's sure speech
Is the pigeon free of messages
Is the whisper of prisoners under guard
Is the marriage of less to more
Is the nugget from the lost mine
Is the bottles after the party
Is the mirror on the door
Is the cat's signature
Is anything but this
Find it

Bard of Short Horizons

What good does it do
  To reach out for fame?
Of friends, just a few
  Will feed my small flame.

For here all I do
  Is give a bare sense
Of what might ensue
  Should talking commence.

To give this full justice,
  I also should mention—
Still want to get published
  To kick-start attention.

Frescos

In rituals for courage in the hunt,
   An artist from our Neolithic past
      Would paint wild beasts against a dark cave wall.

Myself, to keep resolve from going blunt,
   Take baleful forms that float up from the vast
      And etch them on the chambers of my skull.

Born into milder times, those *I* confront—
   The monsters I should conquer and outlast—
      Are deadly as their lion or their bull.

For here, where everyone bears evil's brunt,
   I wield weak words to help me to hold fast
      Against stupidity's relentless pull.

When reason's served to feed insanity,
   And virtue lawyers immorality,
      Our only quarry is reality.

Crispin's Quandary

For all the dragons that you bravely smote,
To them it doesn't matter what you wrote.

And though your speech may coruscate with wit,
Your listeners—they're having none of it.

They'd rather wait for opportunity
To cash in clichés with impunity

Or sit risk-free in front of some sized screen
And nod with no one asking what they mean.

"Well good for them!" is what you'd like to say,
And wave goodbye to cheer them on their way.

But be it curse or just psychology,
You can't, hard as you try, set yourself free.

Though they look off or listen with blank eyes
The more you try to offer fresh surprise—

If you were not enticed
                              to have them understand,
The ink would freeze to ice,
                              the pen fall from your hand.

Co-Creation

A friend is forever.
A friend is an ever-
Interlocutor.

My thought requires your mind,
As eye does light – or blind.
Each word, bespoke-designed.

The sun will draw the rain
Up through the sunflower's vein;
A face makes feelings plain.

The tangled web inside my head,
Unspun as if cocoon's fine thread.
Thus has my dark confusion fled.

Quest

Someone has to fall upon the earth's full breast
And seize it with an infant's gluttony,
Must feel the gentle sun upon him rest

    As antidote to life's monotony.

Sweet rain must fall to wash the agony
Away, the pain of Yahweh's jealous curse,
The stain of Adam's prideful malady,

    The plague of headlights hard behind the hearse.

A flake of fire kidnapped by the wind?
An ember racing through an endless fuse?
Which fate have I the power to rescind

    So I might shout love louder than the news?

I say my story must some way descend
From mom's dawn joyfulness, dad's evening blues.
What place do I begin, where do they end?

    Or do they? Do they if I tell it true?

Quietus

Should we gain access to our thought,
We'd find it isn't what it ought
To be—or not to be—mad Hamlet's question:
To speak or yield to soul's incarceration.

Sometimes gravediggers have been heard to say
That in the act of putting us away,
Before the coffin's lid is nailed down shut,
The phrases throttled our whole life erupt.

To hush this roar before they go insane,
They shovel till the outcry is contained.
So revolution whispered by the pen
Is blocked from passage through the throats of men.

Poet's Lament

When you're chock-full of things to say
And no one cocks an ear and listens,
And even when you kneel to pray,
God keeps His counsel from a distance—

You realize then that people write
In desperation to be heard.
In silent rooms by dim lamplight,
Black ink's the grave where thought's interred.

As if a bird could be enticed
To scratch the ground instead of singing,
Or lovers might be satisfied
With texting in the place of clinging.

Look hard, you'll see I've demonstrated
How loneliness can be placated.

Dreamcatchers

I catch the dream before it fades
And pin it to a waiting page,
This reed my ready instrument
To ward off ego's rough intent.

For will will want to have its say,
Will curve the word toward its one way
And herd the wildlife mind invents
To huddle in its narrow tents.

If you awoke within your dream
Would you build dams against the stream
Of worlds that flow from nature's soul,
Afraid of what you can't control?

Brave poets like spear fishermen
Lean over voids with their mere pen.

Clinician's Petition

I wish someone would do for me
What in my work I do for others
And try to see the world I see,
Since no one's life is like another's.

Or I might wish that I were free
Of yearning for a band of brothers,
Stop reaching for that harmony
One rarely even finds in lovers.

I'd not then need to extricate
Myself from bonds of family,
Or transmute apathy's checkmate
To love—with foolish alchemy.

I hold an ace card on my side:
While writing I'm anesthetized.

what is your story

I don't know your story
you are invisible
you have no reflection
the story sleeps
does not awaken
to the questioner's
command
you say you are my friend
you want to know my mind
my mind the knit of stories
what is your mind
what are your stories
you are invisible to me
grit of blown sand
you don't reflect the light
I don't know your story
light and darkness have their story
the sea bridges their yearning
I don't know your story
where is your light
where is your darkness
you want to be my friend
friends are sides to a story
I don't know your story
listen to the day
whisper to the night
I don't know your story
you want my story
where will I go
to be a story
if not to you
I don't know your story

here is the key
how easily
it enters the lock
I don't know your story
you ask for my story
you want to be my friend
I don't know your story

Publish the Poet

"Publisher, publisher, publish the poet
So he won't have to bother his friends.
Be he good, be he bad, expose it and show it,
He'll hunt us, confront us, and bug us till then.

　"Publisher, publisher, lighten our burden
　Of making his ego more bold and less hurtin'."

"I 'pologize," the publisher replied,
"But though your situation is heart-rending,
I've stamped 'Denied!' upon the tears I cried.
It's world, not poet here, that needs defending.

　"Take heart, your sacrifice goes not unnoticed.
　Your medals are forthcoming from the POTUS."

Envoi

Song to Sing

This song of despair is only my own,
Sang bird of the forest, singing alone,
But if it should reach your listening ear,
Sing out in response so I know you are near.

Don't pity the bird who sings so forlorn,
But pity the form in which you were born,
That you're not a bird who cries out his heart,
Have no song to sing when driven apart

From lovers and family, friends you have known,
Have no song to sing in the forest alone.

Phoenix

How much the dream proves greater than a man
Can make—a miracle of light from dark,
A world from naught, creation without plan,
Fact kindling for imagination's spark.

And so I thought as desperately I clutched
The hope of something living past my death.
It's not a cripple's place to spurn a crutch.
Beginning, word—at end, stripped to its breath.

And then I thought of you, our woodland walks.
You helped me find and look to cure my blindness,
To reach the limit of all need for talk,
Replacing it with hunger for your kindness.

The knot Borromean guards unity,
With me and we and love its Trinity.